Writing Research Papers

New, Revised Edition

Your complete guide to the process of writing a research paper, from finding a topic to preparing the final manuscript

McDougal Littell
A HOUGHTON MIFFLIN COMPANY

Evanston, Illinois ▪ Boston ▪ Dallas

Special thanks to Ann Gallagher and Maureen Kelly-Burke of Rockport High
School for their help in verifying the suitability of these materials for the
classroom.

These materials were prepared by Robert D. Shepherd, a licensed teacher of English
in the states of Massachusetts and New Hampshire; an educational writer,
researcher, and consultant; and a senior partner in Wordworks Publishing Services.

With minor exceptions, this book follows the style for documentation set forth in
the *MLA Handbook for Writers of Research Papers.* Documentation style for some
recent technologies, including online computer services, has been updated.

The editors have made every effort to trace the ownership of the copyrighted
materials found in this book. Any information that would lead to finding sources of
unacknowledged materials used in the book would be greatly appreciated.

ISBN 0–395–79962–7

1 2 3 4 5 6 7 8 9 – DCI – 01 00 99 98 97 96

Contents

APPENDIX Ⓐ
Computers and the Research Paper................................*77*

APPENDIX Ⓑ
Abbreviations for Use in Research Papers..................*79*

APPENDIX Ⓒ
Forms for Working Bibliography and Works Cited Entries......*82*

APPENDIX Ⓓ
Alternative Documentation Styles...........................*91*

Index *112*

Research as Exploration and Discovery

Research is about satisfying curiosity, about finding something you are interested in, exploring it, and making discoveries. Research is about extending the range of what you know. It is like sailing off the edge of the map into unknown territory. Research is an exciting adventure, but this adventure requires no fancy equipment. All you really need is curiosity, a desire to find out *who, what, where, when, why,* and *how.*

Types of Research

There are two major kinds of research, primary and secondary. **Primary research** involves generating new ideas and information on your own. If you take a note pad into the woods, watch the animals there, and take notes on what you see, that is primary research. If you make up a questionnaire and ask people to answer the questions, that is also primary research. Other examples of primary research are

- Conducting an experiment and recording the results.

- Searching through documents at a county courthouse to discover your family history.

- Interviewing someone about his or her personal experiences.

- Reading a novel and taking notes on your personal responses to it.

Secondary research involves gathering together and analyzing the results of other people's primary research. Suppose, for example, that you want to learn about life in the Cherokee town of Tenasi before the Europeans came to North America. All that you know to begin with is that the name of the town gave us the name of the state Tennessee. To find out more about the topic, you could do secondary research. You could read books and

> **"**Research is about satisfying curiosity, about finding something you are interested in, exploring it, and making discoveries.**"**

1

articles written about Tenasi, or you could interview historians who have done research on the subject. Most of the work that you will do when you write your research paper will probably be secondary research.

Why Do Research Papers?

Research can be fascinating and glamorous. After all, it is the main activity of most writers, reporters, historians, and scientists. However, research can also be a practical, everyday sort of activity, one useful to people with jobs that are less exotic. Restaurant managers do research to find out what their customers might like. Students do research to find out about careers. Whatever you plan to do with your future, knowing how to do research will be of great value to you, and there is no better introduction to doing research than planning and writing a research paper.

Research is like sailing off the edge of the map into unknown territory.

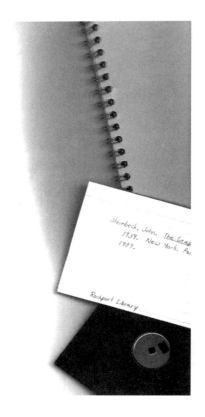

Understanding the Research Paper

Have you ever written a report that drew from several different sources? If so, you have already produced something like a research paper. A research paper is a written report that presents the results of a purposeful, focused, in-depth study of a specific topic. Its writer chooses a topic, gathers information about the topic from several different sources, and then presents that information in an organized way.

Writing a research paper will most likely be the most time-consuming and challenging task that you have ever undertaken as a student. However, do not let the size of the task scare you. You will find researching your paper quite easy if you take it one step at a time, following the guidelines in this book.

Research and the Writing Process

Some types of writing, like taking notes in class or jotting down a grocery list, are done at one time. However, most types of writing are done over a period of time. In other words, writing is a process, and it can be roughly divided into stages—prewriting, drafting, revising, proofreading, and publishing. This book will take you through the following activities in the process of writing a research paper:

The Research Process

- Choosing your subject
- Doing preliminary research
- Limiting your subject to a specific topic

> *"Don't let the size of the task scare you. You will find researching and writing your paper quite easy if you take it one step at a time, following the guidelines in this book."*

> *" Writing is a process, and it can be roughly divided into stages—prewriting, drafting, revising, proofreading, and publishing. "*

The Research Process (cont.)

- Finding an angle and writing a statement of controlling purpose

- Preparing a list of possible sources (a Working Bibliography)

- Taking notes and developing a rough, or working, outline

- Organizing your notes and making a final outline

- Writing your first draft

- Revising your draft

- Writing the final draft with a complete list of Works Cited

As you work through the next few chapters, you will come to understand more clearly what constitutes a successful research paper. For now, read the sample research paper on the following pages. Then answer the questions at the end of the paper.

Mother and two children on road at Tule Lake, California, September, 1939. Photo by Dorothea Lange, courtesy of The Library of Congress.

Maika Carlos-Díaz

Ms. Lee

Junior English

13 May 1993

The Political Message of John Steinbeck's

<u>The Grapes of Wrath</u>

A novel, like a movie, is a form of entertainment. However, some novels do a great deal more than entertain. Some pack a powerful political message. For example, <u>Uncle Tom's Cabin</u>, by Harriet Beecher Stowe, created controversy from the moment it was published. <u>The Jungle</u>, by Upton Sinclair, alerted the country to the horrors of the meatpacking industry.

John Steinbeck's <u>The Grapes of Wrath</u> is another example of a novel with a powerful political message. It warned that exploitation of migrant workers would cause them to rise up as a group against their oppressors, the state and the wealthy landowners. But beyond that, the novel shows how such an oppressive situation can result in a profound philosophical change in the people who experience it.

The following pages examine the political and philosophical message in Steinbeck's novel. First they explain the historical and economic situation to which Steinbeck was reacting. Then they present Steinbeck's opinions about that situation. Finally, they show how the events in the novel reflect Steinbeck's beliefs about both the political and the human changes that can result from continued oppression.

<u>The Grapes of Wrath</u> is an historical novel, "a summation of national experience at a given time" (Levant 93). Therefore, to understand the novel, one must understand the historical events on which it was based. The historical and

---

First paragraph presents some background information to provide a context for the thesis statement.

Thesis statement

This paragraph helps the reader to get his or her bearings by outlining the argument to be presented in the rest of the paper.

Titles of long works are underlined.

This is the standard form for parenthetical documentation. The author's last name is followed by the page number or numbers.

economic experience that Steinbeck was reacting to was that of the migrants who left the Oklahoma Dust Bowl in the late 1930s ("Dust Bowl"). In Oklahoma, storms blew away topsoil (Frazier 204), covered pastures, and suffocated livestock (Tannehill 7). At the time, the country was in the grip of a severe economic downturn called the Great Depression ("Great Depression"). Crop failure, added to already low crop prices, "led to the foreclosure of many small farms and the subsequent homelessness of many farm families" (Frazier 204).

Between 300,000 and 400,000 homeless farmers from the Dust Bowl area packed their possessions into old cars or trucks and headed to California to find work (Stein 216). The panhandle region of Oklahoma and Texas lost more than half its residents. However, when these people got to California, they did not find the paradise they were looking for. They found "not a Promised Land but a man-blighted Eden" (Crockett 195). As one Oklahoma refugee put it in a song,

> Lots of folks back East, they say, leavin' home every
>   day.
> Beatin' that hot, ole, dusty way to the California
>   line.
> 'Cross the desert sands they roll, gettin' out of the
>   ole Dust Bowl,
> Thinkin' they're goin' to a sugar bowl, but here is
>   what they find:
> . . . .
> California's a Garden of Eden, a paradise to live in
>   or see,
> But believe it or not, you won't find it so hot,
> If you ain't got the Do-Re-Me.   (Guthrie)

Most of the migrants who arrived in California didn't have any "Do-Re-Me," or money. When they arrived, they camped

The writer uses a combination of quotations, paraphrases, and summaries to support her points.

The first section of this paper, the part that tells about the historical background of the novel, is arranged chronologically, in time order.

Indent a quotation of more than four lines ten spaces from the left margin. Leave two character spaces at the end of the quotation. Then give the parenthetical citation.

The line of dots shows that one or more complete lines has been left out of the middle of a poem or, in this case, a song.

6

out and looked for work in California's fruit and cotton fields
(Stein 210).

These immigrants discovered that California agriculture
was based on enormous farms, or "factories in the field"
(McWilliams 42).   These farms were "cultivated by migratory
laborers who miraculously turned up for the harvest and
disappeared once the crops were laid by" (Stein 205).

The immigrants from Oklahoma swelled the numbers of
California's migrant labor force and drove wages down (Stein
213-24).   Wages were so low, and jobs were so few, that
thousands of migrants were driven to desperate poverty.   The
extent of the desperation is made clear in a report written in
1939, the year that <u>The Grapes of Wrath</u> was published:

> The State Relief Administration estimates that most
> agricultural workers only have employment for six
> months in the year or less; and that the average
> yearly earnings per family . . . [were] $289 in 1935.
> In the same study the S.R.A. estimated that each
> family . . . should have had at least $780 to eke out
> an existence. . . .   In 1932 there were 181
> agricultural workers for every 100 jobs offered; in
> . . . 1934, 142.   (McWilliams 48)

In other words, the migrant workers were attempting to live on
less than half what they needed just to survive, there were
far more workers than there were jobs, and what few jobs there
were disappeared entirely for half of each year.

Unable to find work, scorned and hounded from place to
place, the migrants from Oklahoma gathered together in
settlements along highways, places that became known as
Hoovervilles, after President Herbert Hoover.   An actress who
visited one of these camps wrote, "I went around in a sick
daze for hours after witnessing unimaginable suffering" (qtd.

No paragraph
indention is necessary
if the quoted material
is one paragraph or
less.

in Stein 219). These settlements were full of hunger and disease. According to historian Walter Stein, "By 1937, the [Oklahoma migrants] had become a local embarrassment, by 1938 a state concern, and by 1939, with the publication of <u>The Grapes of Wrath</u>, a national scandal" (216).

Steinbeck's reaction to the migrants and their situation paralleled the comments of the actress who visited the camp. However, despite being angered and disturbed by the migrants' plight, Steinbeck was reluctant to write about it. When <u>Life</u> magazine asked him to write about the migrants, he declined, saying that he didn't want to profit from the migrants' misery. Later, though, Steinbeck wrote a series of newspaper articles to draw attention to the migrants' problems. Steinbeck actually followed the trail of the Oklahoma migrants and visited their camping places (French, "What Did" 51-52). He also made friends with Tom Collins, who ran a federal relief camp for the migrants.   From Collins, he learned as much as he could about the migrants' lives (Demott xxvii-xxviii). Steinbeck later told an interviewer, "I know what I was talking about [in <u>The Grapes of Wrath</u>]. I lived, off and on, with those [migrants] for . . . three years" (Cameron 19).

In 1938, the year before he published <u>The Grapes of Wrath</u>, Steinbeck wrote a nonfiction pamphlet about the migrants. This pamphlet made Steinbeck's opinions about the migrant situation very clear. Entitled <u>Their Blood Is Strong</u>, the pamphlet told about the horrible conditions of the migrants' lives. Steinbeck wrote in the pamphlet that the migrants' camps were full of sickness--of pneumonia, measles, tuberculosis, rickets, and pellagra (89). The migrants also faced an even more terrible problem:

If the name of the author of the source is given in the text of the paper, then the citation need include only the page number.

This paragraph begins the second section of the paper, which discusses Steinbeck's reactions to the migrant situation.

Generally speaking, each major section of a research paper should begin with such a transitional paragraph, one that presents the main idea of the section.

Brackets can be used to add necessary information to a quotation, but make sure that the added material does not change the meaning of the quotation.

8

> There has been no war in California, no plague, no
> bombing of open towns and roads, no shelling of
> cities. It is a beautiful year. And thousands of
> families are starving. . . .
>
>   [It's] in the tents you see along the roads and in
>   the shacks built from dump heap materials that the
>   hunger is, and it isn't malnutrition. It is
>   starvation. (88)

In his pamphlet, Steinbeck went beyond describing
existing conditions. He also warned that terrible anger was
building among the migrants:

> Dignity is all gone, and [their] spirit has turned to
> sullen anger. . . . We regard this destruction of
> dignity . . . as one of the most regrettable results
> of the migrant's life, since it does . . . make [of
> the migrant] a sullen outcast who will strike
> at our government in any way that occurs to him.
> (62, 70)

Steinbeck repeated this warning several times in the
pamphlet. He wrote, for example, that the mistreatment of the
migrants "constitutes a criminal endangering of the peace of
the state" (69). In another place in the pamphlet he said
that California "is gradually building a human structure
[migrant labor] which will certainly change the state, and may
. . . destroy the present system of agricultural economics"
(59). So it was Steinbeck's opinion that the migrant
situation was explosive and might lead to insurrection against
the government.

The Grapes of Wrath elaborates on and puts into story
form the political warning that Steinbeck made in his pamphlet
Their Blood Is Strong. In the novel Steinbeck shows how
oppression inevitably turns nonpolitical people into political

When quoting more
than one paragraph,
indent all full
paragraphs in the
quotation an
additional three
spaces.

Both the author and
the title of the source
of this quotation are
mentioned in the text,
so all that is needed is
the page number.

When quoted material
appears in the source
on nonconsecutive
pages, give the first
page number, a
comma, and then the
number of the page on
which the material is
continued.

This paragraph
introduces the third
section of the paper,
which discusses the
political message of
the novel.

people. It drives them to join with others who are oppressed. When that happens, a group emerges, and a group is a potentially potent force. But the novel also elaborates on this change by showing that it is accompanied by a philosophical shift from a self-centered focus on the individual to a focus on people as a community.

The novel shows the political and philosophical evolution of the migrants through the story of a single migrant family, the Joads. At the beginning of the novel, the Joads, like most of the displaced farmers of that era, see themselves as helpless victims of natural and economic events beyond their control. They feel powerless to fight against the system that is running people off their land. One tenant farmer, searching for someone to blame for the loss of his farm, considers blaming the tractor driver who is knocking his house down. But the tractor driver is just taking orders from the bank. The bank has a president and a board of directors, but they are just taking orders from the East. The people in the East are just responding to economic events. No one is really responsible or in charge (49; ch. 5). In this early historical chapter, Steinbeck is setting the stage for the seemingly overwhelming odds that the Joads must face.

Having lost their land, the Joads look for a simple solution that will make everything all right. They have seen handbills from California, promising lots of work and high wages (117; ch. 10). California therefore becomes the promised land. Ma Joad dreams of getting a little white house in California, surrounded by orange trees (118; ch. 10). Grampa Joad dreams of picking "a wash tub full of grapes" and sitting down in it (119; ch. 10). The family sees California as a kind of paradise, and the symbol of this paradise is its fruit (Crockett 195). At this point the Joads

When referring to a literary work that is available in different editions or from different publishers, give the line numbers (for short works) or chapter numbers (for long works like novels) or act, scene, and line numbers (for plays). The reader of the paper can then find the source no matter what edition he or she is using.

have still not taken responsibility for improving their
situation.   Instead, they simply set out for an Eden.

However, paradise turns out not to be so easily
attainable.   Steinbeck shows how on their arrival in
California the Joads, and others like them, can begin a change
from a naive, resigned unit to a thoughtful, questioning group
of individuals.   In California the Joads meet a father and a
son who warn them that California is not a paradise.   The
father points out that the land is all owned by large
companies.   People go hungry while land lies fallow, or
unworked, because "ever'thing in California is owned" (264-65;
ch. 18).   This is the first stage of the Joads' political
education.   However, the Joads have no choice but to ignore
the warning and go on.

In Hooverville, a roadside migrant settlement that the
Joads pass through, Steinbeck shows the migrants' dawning
anger and their first hesitant steps toward rebellion.   A young
man named Floyd explains to Tom the foolhardiness of coming to
California on the strength of a handbill advertising work.
Floyd explains that the wealthy landowners in California send
out thousands of handbills to attract a surplus of crop
pickers.   The workers then compete with one another and drive
wages down.   Tom suggests to Floyd the possibility of
organized resistance:

>   Tom said angrily, "Them peaches got to be
> picked right now, don't they?   Jus' when they're
> ripe?"
>
>   "'Course they do."
>
>   "Well, s'pose them people got together an' says,
> 'Let 'em rot.'   Wouldn' be long 'fore the price went
> up, by God!"

However, Floyd points out that whenever anyone tries to become a leader, he is simply jailed or killed, and his family also suffers (315-17; ch. 20).

But despite the warning, Tom Joad has begun to change. In the beginning of the novel, he is portrayed as someone concerned only with himself and his own immediate affairs. Statements such as "I'm jus' puttin' one foot in front a the other" and "I climb fences when I got fences to climb" demonstrate this point (223-24; ch. 16). However, in Hooverville Tom risks his own neck to protect Floyd from a deputy. By sticking one foot in front of the deputy and tripping him when the deputy is about to arrest Floyd for being a "red," Tom begins his transformation into a political and involved person (339-40; ch. 20). For the first time, Tom takes an active role and sees the need to reach out and help another person.

Tom's mother, too, starts to think politically, and beyond herself. As the Joads leave Hooverville, they are confronted by an angry mob of locals who have come to burn down the camp. Tom evades them, and Ma says defiantly, "They ain't gonna wipe us out. . . . A different time's comin'" (360; ch. 20). Through these two characters, Steinbeck is showing that the passive, helpless migrants of the Dust Bowl evolve as thinking individuals as they assess their life experiences.

The Joads' next stop is Weedpatch, a government camp for migrants. There Steinbeck presents the idea that the migrants can learn that good things are indeed possible if people work together for a common cause. At Weedpatch there are no policemen. The people live together in dignity. Timothy Wallace, a migrant at the camp who helps Tom find a job, describes Weedpatch in this way:

> This here camp is a organization. People there look
> out for theirselves. Got the nicest strang band in
> these parts. Got a little charge account in the
> store for folks that's hungry. Fi' dollars--you can
> git that much food an' the camp'll stan' good. We
> ain't never had no trouble with the law. I guess the
> big farmers is scairt of that. Can't throw us in
> jail--why, it scares 'em. Figger maybe if we can
> gove'n ourselves, maybe we'll do other things. (382;
> ch. 22)

Tom and other men in the camp successfully organize to
stop a plan to cause a riot at Weedpatch. Through Weedpatch
the Joads learn that the concept of organized resistance, first
introduced at Hooverville, can be successfully executed for
the good of the community. Pa Joad points out, "They's change
a-comin'. I don' know what. Maybe we won't live to see her.
But she's a-comin'. They's a res'less feelin'" (443; ch. 24).

Outside the peace of Weedpatch, however, a corrupt system
is still feeding the migrants' anger. In order for the
agricultural associations to keep food prices high, the excess
fruit is destroyed or goes to waste. Steinbeck's account of
sickness in migrant camps in Their Blood Is Strong seems to
echo in the fruit imagery:

> Carloads of oranges dumped on the ground. . . . A
> million people hungry, needing the fruit. . . . And
> the smell of rot fills the country. . . . And
> children dying of pellagra must die because a profit
> cannot be taken from an orange. And coroners must
> fill in the certificates--died of malnutrition--because
> the food must rot, must be forced to rot. (448-49;
> ch. 25)

Steinbeck makes the effect of this waste on the migrants clear: "[I]n the eyes of the hungry there is a growing wrath. In the souls of the people the grapes of wrath are filling and growing heavy, growing heavy for the vintage" (449; ch. 25).

Steinbeck's reference to wrath points to the significance of the title, The Grapes of Wrath, which in turn shows his belief in the transforming power of the migrants' anger. The immediate source of the title is the first stanza of "The Battle Hymn of the Republic," a song of the Civil War era by Julia Ward Howe:

> Mine eyes have seen the glory of the coming of the
>> Lord;
> He is trampling out the vintage where the
>> grapes of wrath are stored. . . .
> (Familiar Quotations 566)

Steinbeck's novel is also a battle hymn, but one about the issue of migrant labor rather than the issue of slavery. In addition to Howe's song, there is another source for Steinbeck's title. In the Bible, the Revelation of St. John mentions "the wine of wrath" forced upon people by a "Babylon" that is "fallen" (Rev. 14.8; Crockett 195). Babylon was an ancient city-state described in the Bible as a wicked place. In his title Steinbeck seems to be suggesting that the migrants, having learned to think of themselves as part of a group, might draw upon their anger and rise up to overthrow the Babylon, or state, that has mistreated them so horribly. The wine of their wrath will cause Babylon to fall. That's just what Steinbeck had predicted in his pamphlet Their Blood Is Strong.

Contrasting with Weedpatch is another of the Joads' stops--the Pixley camp, a place run by the Hooper ranch, a large agricultural concern. Conditions are terrible, and when the pay drops to 2.5 cents a day, the Joads face real hunger (491; ch. 26). In Pixley, the owners of the camp employ armed guards who patrol the place, including the movement of its residents (473-74; ch. 26).

The climactic event of the novel occurs when Tom's friend Casy, who has actively tried to organize resistance to the system, is killed by a deputy. Tom kills the deputy and is forced into hiding (495-99; ch. 26). He has now risked everything and sees the full potential of organized resistance. As Tom says to his mother, "I been a-wonderin' why we can't do that all over. Throw out the cops that ain't our people. All work together for our own thing . . ." (536; ch. 28). Tom then commits himself to working, as Casy did, as a labor organizer.

Similarly, the men around him are changing. Steinbeck extends his theme of change and transformation by showing migrants gathering together and turning their mistreatment into anger:

> The women watched the men, watched to see whether
> the break had come at last. The women stood silently
> and watched. And where a number of men gathered
> together, the fear went from their faces, and anger
> took its place. And the women sighed with relief,
> for they knew it was all right--the break had not
> come; and the break would never come as long as fear
> could turn to wrath.
>
> Tiny points of grass came through the earth, and
> in a few days the hills were pale green with the
> beginning year. (556; ch. 29)

Springtime and green grass are traditional symbols of rebirth and renewal. This passage seems to suggest that when the migrants gather as a group, they become angry. This gathering signals the beginning of a new world for them, and perhaps an end to the world of their oppressors.

The change in the migrants goes beyond a purely political one, however. They have also learned to reach out to one another, to become one family. For example, when Tom decides to become a labor organizer, he no longer worries about himself and his own affairs. In fact, when Ma wonders aloud whether Tom might be killed as a result of his organizing activities, he replies:

> "Well, maybe like Casy says, a fella ain't got a soul of his own, but on'y a piece of a big one--an' then----"
>
> "Then what, Tom?"
>
> "Then it don' matter. Then I'll be all aroun' in the dark. I'll be ever'where--wherever you look. Wherever they's a fight so hungry people can eat, I'll be there. Wherever they's a cop beatin' up a guy, I'll be there. If Casy knowed, why, I'll be in the way guys yell when they're mad an'--I'll be in the way kids laugh when they're hungry an' they know supper's ready. An' when our folks eat the stuff they raise an' live in the houses they build--why, I'll be there. See?" (537; ch. 28)

Tom has learned to think of himself as part of a larger group of oppressed people like himself. His own welfare and the welfare of the group have merged.

Ma also has gone through a transformation. In the early part of the novel, Ma is concerned only with her immediate family. For instance, during the family's trip to California, she says, "All we got is the family unbroke" (219; ch. 16). In other words, people beyond the family can't be counted on. Near the end of the novel, though, Ma shows how completely she

has changed her point of view. She says directly that the
family used to be her primary concern but that now she cares
about people in general: "Use' ta be the fambly was fust. It
ain't so now. It's anybody. Worse off we get, the more we
got to do" (569; ch. 30).

Ma, like her son Tom, has learned to see herself not as
an isolated person or as a member of an isolated family but
rather as a member of the human family. And this, Steinbeck
seems to imply, is the power of the people. Their resistance
has become not just a political cause, but a powerful moral
one as well.

The Grapes of Wrath presents in story form Steinbeck's
reading of the migrant situation. In his novel Steinbeck
warns about the explosiveness of the migrant situation by
showing how members of one migrant family become politicized.
In the conclusion of his novel and in its title, Steinbeck
suggests that the migrants have become a cohesive group driven
by anger.

By showing how the Joads come to worry about people other
than themselves, Steinbeck is showing, as he did in Their
Blood Is Strong, that the mistreatment of the migrants will
bind them together into a politically powerful group. That
group, Steinbeck affirms, may threaten the government and the
economic system that has oppressed them, but the threat is
based on an unshakable sense of community and morality. As Ma
suggests in the novel and in the conclusion of the film version
of The Grapes of Wrath, the human spirit is unbreakable:
"We'll go on forever. . . . We're the people."

The conclusion of the
paper is presented in
two paragraphs. The
writer begins her
conclusion by restating
her thesis in different
words.

Works Cited

Newspaper article reprinted in another source

Cameron, Tom. "The Grapes of Wrath Author Guards Self from Threats at Moody Gulch." Los Angeles Times 9 July 1939: 1-2. Rpt. in Conversations with John Steinbeck. Ed. Thomas Fensch. Jackson: UP of Mississippi, 1988. 19-20.

Journal article

Crockett, H. Kelly. "The Bible and The Grapes of Wrath." College English 24 (1962): 193-99.

Introduction to a book edited by the writer of the introduction

Demott, Robert. Introduction. Working Days: The Journals of The Grapes of Wrath: 1938-1941. Ed. Demott. New York: Viking-Penguin, 1989. xxi-lvii.

Online computer information service

"Dust Bowl." Academic American Encyclopedia. Online. Prodigy. 31 May 1992.

Collection (The same piece could be listed by editor or compiler if you wish to emphasize that information.)

Familiar Quotations: A Collection of Passages, Phrases and Proverbs Traced to Their Sources in Ancient and Modern Literature. Comp. John Bartlett. Ed. Emily Morrison Beck. 15th ed. Boston: Little, 1980. 566.

Frazier, Thomas R., ed. Since 1865. 2nd ed. New York: Harcourt, 1978. Vol. 2 of The Underside of American History: Other Readings. 2 vols. 1971-78.

French, Warren, ed. A Companion to The Grapes of Wrath. New York: Viking, 1963.

Three hyphens used to indicate another work by the same person

---. "What Did John Steinbeck Know About the 'Okies'?" French, Companion 51-53.

Movie

The Grapes of Wrath. Screenplay by Nunnally Johnson. Dir. John Ford. Perf. John Carradine, Jane Darwell, and Henry Fonda. Twentieth Century-Fox, 1940.

Online computer information service

"The Great Depression." Compton's Online Encyclopedia. Online. America Online. 30 May 1992.

Recording

Guthrie, Woody. "Do-Re-Me." Dust Bowl Ballads. Compact disc. Rounder, 1988.

Levant, Howard.   "The Fully Matured Art: The Grapes of Wrath."
     The Novels of John Steinbeck: A Critical Study.
     Columbia: U of Missouri P, 1974.   93-129.

McWilliams, Carey.   "The End of a Cycle."   Factories in the
     Field.   Boston: Little, 1939.   305-25.   Rpt. in French,
     Companion 42-49.

Stein, Walter J.   "The Okie Impact."   California and the Dust
     Bowl Migration.   Westport: Greenwood, 1973.   32-64.   Rpt.
     in Frazier, 205-34.

Steinbeck, John.   The Grapes of Wrath.   1939.   New York:
     Penguin, 1976.

---.   Their Blood Is Strong.   San Francisco: Lubin, 1938.
     Rpt. in French, Companion 53-92.

Tannehill, Ivan Ray.   "Dusters and Black Blizzards."   Drought:
     Its Causes and Effects.   Princeton: Princeton UP, 1948.
     10-12, 44-51.   Rpt. in French, Companion 5-8.

Work in a collection

Republished work. Note that the date of first publication is given after the title.

Migrant woman and children. Photo by Dorothea Lange, courtesy of The Library of Congress.

19

Think and Respond

In your learning log, in your writing folder, or in a group discussion, analyze the sample research paper on the previous pages. Respond to these questions about the paper:

1. What information appears in the heading of the paper? At the top of each page?

2. What is the main idea, or thesis, of the paper? Does the writer support her thesis? How?

3. What are the three major parts of the body of the paper? What is the main idea of each part? Does the order of the parts make sense? Why, or why not?

4. How does the writer of the paper indicate, within the paper, that she has taken material from a source?

5. Where does the writer's complete list of sources appear, and what is it called?

6. Does the writer use a wide variety of sources? What different kinds of sources does she use?

7. How does the writer introduce her paper?

8. How does the writer conclude her paper?

9. Does the writer use evidence skillfully to support the claims that she makes? Give two examples.

10. What suggestions for improvement might you give to this writer if you had a chance to do so?

Migrants camped by a roadside. Photo by Dorothea Lange, courtesy of The Library of Congress.

Discovering a Topic for Research

2

One of the most important parts of doing a research paper is choosing a topic. By choosing wisely, you can ensure that your research will go smoothly and that you will enjoy doing it.

Choosing a Subject That You Care About

A **subject** is a broad area of interest, such as African-American history or astronomy or sports. One way to approach the search for a research paper topic is first to choose a general area of interest and then to focus on some part of it. Make sure that you have a real reason for wanting to explore the subject. Often the best subjects for research papers are ones that are related to your own life or to the lives of people you know.

If you are already keeping a writing ideas section in your journal or in your writing portfolio, you can refer to that list for possible subjects. If you are not regularly listing your writing ideas, you might consider starting to do so now.

You can begin exploring general subject areas that interest you by completing the following Interest Inventory:

> "Often the best subjects for research papers are ones that are directly related to your own life or to the lives of people you know."

Interest Inventory

Respond in writing to the following items:

1. What activities do I enjoy?
2. What subjects do I enjoy reading about?
3. What books have I enjoyed reading in the past?

> " If I could have a long conversation with someone from any place and from any time in history, who would that person be? "

4. What subjects from my classes have captured my attention and interest?

5. What questions do I really want to know the answers to? (Write six questions, beginning with the words *who, what, where, when, why,* and *how.*)

6. What commonplace things are complete mysteries to me? What ordinary things, such as a sunset, a nuclear reactor, a computer hard drive, a human heart, flight, or diving gear, would I like to understand more completely?

7. What interesting careers or hobbies do my friends, acquaintances, or relatives have? What interesting experiences have they had?

8. If I could have a long conversation with someone from any place and from any time in history, who would that person be?

If your answers to the Interest Inventory questions don't suggest a general subject area that you would like to learn more about, try the following activities:

Searching for a Subject

1. Spend some time in a library, simply walking up and down the aisles or browsing through the card catalog, looking for subjects that appeal to you.

2. Browse through encyclopedias, almanacs, atlases, dictionaries, or recent periodical indexes. Useful indexes include the *Readers' Guide to Periodical Literature* and the *Humanities Index.*

3. Glance at the tables of contents of your textbooks, looking for subjects that you'd like to know more about.

4. If you have access to an electronic encyclopedia, a knowledge database, or a computer index that covers general subjects, start with an interesting search word, see where that leads, and try the subheadings or cross-references that come up.

5. Watch some public television specials that deal with nature, with science, with travel, with history, or with the future, or listen to some public radio programs that deal with these matters. See if any of the subjects of the programs capture your imagination.

6. Look through news magazines for subjects related to current events.

7. List some novels or stories that you have read recently and think about possible topic ideas related to these. Look through your literature textbook for other possibilities.

> " Spend some time in a library, simply walking up and down the aisles or browsing through the card catalog, looking for subjects that appeal to you. "

Limiting Your Subject/Choosing a Topic

Once you have a **general subject** that you are interested in, such as migrant workers or animal communication, the next step is to narrow that subject to a **specific topic** that can be treated in a research paper.

Doing Preliminary Research

If you already know a great deal about your subject, then you can probably think of a specific topic to research within that subject area. However, if you are not already an expert, it is a good idea to do some preliminary research to identify potential topics. Here are a few suggestions for preliminary research:

Research Tip

Most research paper topics fall into one of four broad categories. You may want to start your topic search by choosing a general subject area under one of these categories:

Language and Literature

Arts and Humanities

History and Social Studies

Science and Mathematics

Throughout the rest of this book you will find a number of Research Tips, like this one, placed in the margins. These tips will provide specific information about research in each of the four general subject areas listed above.

Ideas for Preliminary Research

- Read encyclopedia articles.

- List questions about the subject and interview someone knowledgeable about it.

- Brainstorm with friends, classmates, or relatives to find out what they know about the subject.

- Check the *Readers' Guide to Periodical Literature* to find general articles on your subject.

- Find a textbook that covers the general field of study to which your subject belongs. Read about your subject in that textbook.

- Go to the place in the library where books on the subject are shelved. Choose books at random and look them over.

Here is how one student conducted her preliminary research:

One Student's Process: Maika

When Maika completed her interest inventory, she paused at the question about interesting experiences that relatives have had. Maika's grandfather came from Guatemala by way of Mexico. As a young man, he had been a migrant worker. Surely there were many aspects of her grandfather's experiences or of the culture of his native land that would make interesting topics for a research paper. Maika decided to interview her grandfather about his early experiences.

Using Prewriting Techniques

In addition to conducting preliminary research, you may also be able to come up with a specific topic by using one of the following prewriting techniques:

1. **Freewriting and Clustering.** Write whatever comes to mind about the subject for five minutes, or draw a cluster chart on which you list your topic and related ideas connected by lines.

2. **Brainstorming.** Working with a group of friends or classmates, write down a list of topics that come to mind as people think about the subject.

3. **Questioning.** Write a list of questions about the subject. Begin your questions with the words *who, what, where, when, why,* or *how;* or start your questions with *What if . . .*

4. **Discussion.** Listen to what other students know about your subject, what aspects of it they find intriguing, what difficulties they foresee in researching it, and so on.

Evaluating Possible Topics

Once you have generated a list of possible topic ideas, you need to evaluate them. That is, you need to judge them on the basis of certain criteria. Here are some criteria for judging a research topic:

1. The topic should be interesting. Often the most interesting topics are ones that are related to your family's history, to your future, to your major goals, to the place where you live or would like to live, to a career that interests you, or to a hobby or other activity that you enjoy. The topic might be something that has caught your interest in the past, perhaps something you have read about or have studied in school.

2. The topic should be covered in readily available sources. When considering a topic, always check the card catalogs in a couple of local libraries and the *Readers' Guide to Periodical Literature* to see if sources are available.

> "The topic might be something that has caught your interest in the past, perhaps something you have read about or have studied in school."

3. The topic should be significant. Choose a topic that is significant for you, one worth your time and energy.

4. The topic should be objective. Make sure that your topic is one that can be supported with facts.

5. The topic should not be straight biography, history, reporting, or retelling of a literary work. You should not simply rehash material available in other sources. You should look for a unique angle on or approach to the topic.

6. The topic should be narrow enough to be treated fully. Ask your teacher how many pages you should have in your final product and choose a topic that is narrow enough to be treated in a paper of that length.

Writing a Statement of Controlling Purpose

Once you have decided on a specific topic, your next step is to write a **statement of controlling purpose.** This is a sentence or pair of sentences that tells what you want to accomplish in your paper. It is called a statement of controlling purpose because it controls, or guides, your research. The statement of controlling purpose usually contains one or more key words that tell what the paper is going to accomplish. Key words that often appear in statements of controlling purpose include *analyze, classify, compare, contrast, define, describe, determine, establish, explain, identify, prove,* and *support.*

Here are two examples of statements of controlling purpose:

> The purpose of this paper will be to describe the elements that give the prose writing of Sandra Cisneros a poetic quality.

> The purpose of this paper will be to contrast animal communication and human language to show how they are different.

To come up with a statement of controlling purpose, you will probably have to do a considerable amount of preliminary research. That is because before you can write a statement of controlling purpose, you have to know enough about your topic to have a general idea of what you want to say in your paper. Here is an example of one student's process:

One Student's Process: Maika

Maika's grandfather had been a migrant worker when he first came to California from Guatemala. Maika was interested in learning more about the migrant experience, so she asked her teacher if she knew of any interesting books on the subject. Her teacher recommended John Steinbeck's *The Grapes of Wrath*. Maika read the novel. Then she went to the library and looked up Steinbeck and *The Grapes of Wrath* in the card catalog. She found several collections of critical essays about the novel. As she looked through these essays, she found that several subjects were discussed over and over. She made a list of these subjects:

Steinbeck's characterizations of women

Biblical symbolism in *The Grapes of Wrath*

Steinbeck's theory that people in groups have exceptional powers

The Grapes of Wrath as a political novel

She decided that she would write a paper that would explain the political message of Steinbeck's novel. Her statement of controlling purpose was "The purpose of this paper is to explain the political message of John Steinbeck's *The Grapes of Wrath.*"

> "To come up with a statement of controlling purpose, you will probably have to do a considerable amount of preliminary research."

Here are some sample statements of controlling purpose:

Statements of Controlling Purpose

A controlling purpose can be to . . .

Support (or to argue against) a policy: The purpose of this paper is to persuade people that foreign language instruction should begin in elementary school.

27

Establish (or to prove false) one or more statements of fact:
The purpose of this paper is to prove that tobacco is a harmful and addictive drug.

Determine the relative value of two or more things: The purpose of this paper is to compare solar, wind, and wave energy to determine which is the most reliable, practical, and cost-effective alternative energy source.

Analyze something into its parts and to show how those parts relate to one another: The purpose of this paper is to describe the stages in the television production process and to explain how those stages interrelate.

Define something: The purpose of this paper is to define the phrase *freedom of the press* by explaining the nature of and limits on press freedom under the law.

Explain causes or effects: The purpose of this paper is to explain the various causes of the destruction of Brazil's rain forests.

Establish a cause-effect relationship: The purpose of this paper is to present the scientific evidence that suggests that cigarette smoking causes cancer.

Describe the development of something over time: The purpose of this paper is to describe how rock-and-roll developed from roots in blues, gospel, and country and western music.

Identify and describe a general trend: The purpose of this paper is to show that a major extinction of South American plant and animal species is now occurring.

Classify individual items into groups or categories: The purpose of this paper is to classify African myths into several distinct categories (creation stories, lineage stories, etc.)

Relate a part to a whole: The purpose of this paper is to examine the place of the worm in the ecosystem of a forest.

Compare and/or contrast two subjects to determine their degree of similarity or difference: The purpose of this paper is to compare and contrast the views of nature in the poetry of Emily Dickinson and Robert Frost.

Examine a technique: The purpose of this paper is to examine the use of the technique of allegory in *The Scarlet Letter*, by Nathaniel Hawthorne.

Explain a general concept by means of specific examples: The purpose of this paper is to explain the concept of a paradox through examples from math, language, and art.

Explain the main idea or message of something: The purpose of this paper is to explain the political message of John Steinbeck's *The Grapes of Wrath*.

The list of possible controlling purposes given above is far from complete. So do not worry if the controlling purpose that you come up with does not fall into one of the categories on the list. Do bear in mind that your controlling purpose should be one that is significant to you and, potentially, to your readers.

Bear in mind, as well, that your controlling purpose may change as you do your research. When you begin writing your research paper, you will replace your controlling purpose with a **thesis statement,** a statement of your main idea. The thesis statement will not contain the phrase "the purpose of this paper is." For more information on writing thesis statements, see pages 53–54.

Finding and Recording Your Sources

3

Once you have written a statement of controlling purpose, you are ready to put together a list of potential sources. This list of sources that might be useful to you in writing your paper is called a **Working Bibliography.** You will already have used some sources during your preliminary research, and you will probably want to include some or all of those sources in your Working Bibliography. As you continue to research and draft, you may discover that some of the sources in this initial list are not useful, and you will undoubtedly find new sources to add to the list. Before you decide to add any source to your list, however, make sure to evaluate it. Information on how to evaluate a source can be found on pages 31–32.

Both print and nonprint sources will be available to you, and you will want to take advantage of both. Here are some good places to start looking for information.

1. Other people. People can be a researcher's greatest resource. Consider interviewing a professor from a local college or university, or people who work for businesses, museums, historical societies, or other organizations.

2. Institutions and organizations. Museums, art galleries, dance studios, performing arts centers, schools for the arts, historical societies, and businesses are good sources of information about some topics.

3. The government. Many libraries have special departments that contain government publications. For some topics, you may want to contact town, city, county, state, or federal government offices directly. Listings of government departments and agencies can be found in telephone directories.

4. The library/media center. Remember that a library is more than just a place for housing books. Libraries also contain periodicals, such as newspapers, magazines, and journals, and

> " People can be a researcher's greatest resource. "

most have many nonprint materials, such as audio-cassette tapes, videotapes, CD-ROM discs, computer software, posters, artwork, and pamphlets.

5. Bookstores. For some topics, the latest information can be found at your local bookstore. If you do not find what you are looking for, ask a bookstore employee to look up your subject or author in *Books in Print*.

6. Bibliographies. A **bibliography** is a list of books and other materials about a particular topic. Your reference librarian can point you to general bibliographies that deal with both large and specific subject areas such as chemistry, the humanities, or plays by Shakespeare. You can also look for bibliographic lists in the backs of books about your topic.

7. Online information services. An **online information service,** or **computer information service,** is an information source that can be communicated with by means of a personal computer and a modem. For information about online computer services, see Appendix A on pages 77–78.

8. Reference works. Reference works include almanacs, atlases, bibliographies, dictionaries, encyclopedias, periodical indexes, and thesauruses. You will find these and other such works in the reference department of your library.

9. Other sources. Do not neglect television programs, live theater performances, radio shows, recordings, videotapes, computer software, and other possible sources of information. Many libraries have extensive collections of audiovisual materials of all kinds, on a wide variety of subjects. Make use of these.

Evaluating Possible Sources

After you have located a potential source, you need to decide whether it will be useful to you. The following questions will help you to evaluate your sources:

1. Is the source authoritative? An **authoritative source** is one that can be relied upon to provide accurate information. Consider the reputation of the publication and of the author. Are they well respected?

Research Tip

History and Social Studies

Local government offices can often be useful to people who are doing historical research. For example, a county court clerk's office might be able to help you find copies of deeds, birth records, marriage records, and other such documents.

31

2. Is the source unbiased? An **unbiased source** is one whose author lacks a special interest that would make his or her work unreliable. For example, a newsletter article claiming that there is no relationship between smoking and disease would have to be taken with a grain of salt if written by a lobbyist for a tobacco company.

3. Is it necessary for the source to be up-to-date? For some topics, such as ones that deal with current science or technology, up-to-date sources are essential, so check the date on the copyright page of your source. For other topics, the copyright date may be less important or not important at all. If, for example, you were writing about nineteenth-century pioneer women in Wyoming, then these women's old diaries and letters would be excellent sources.

4. Is the work written at an appropriate level? Some materials are written for children and, although generally accurate, are simplified and may be misleading in some respects. Others are so technical that they can be understood only after years of study.

5. Does the source come highly recommended? One way to evaluate a source is to ask an expert or authority whether the source is reliable. You can also check the bibliography in a reputable source. If a source is listed in a bibliography, then it is probably being recommended by the author or editor who put that bibliography together.

Preparing Bibliography Cards

Every time you find a source that might be useful for your research paper, you need to prepare a **bibliography card** for it. All of your bibliography cards, taken together, make up your **Working Bibliography.**

A bibliography card serves three basic purposes. First, it enables you to find the source again. Second, it enables you to prepare documentation for your paper. **Documentation** is material included in a research paper to tell the sources from which information was taken. Third, it enables you to prepare the list of Works Cited that will appear at the end of your paper. The

Journals and other periodicals are particularly good sources for research in science and mathematics because practicing scientists and mathematicians publish their latest findings in such places.

Works Cited list is a complete record of the sources referred to in the paper. Here is a sample bibliography card:

Bibliography card for a book by a single author

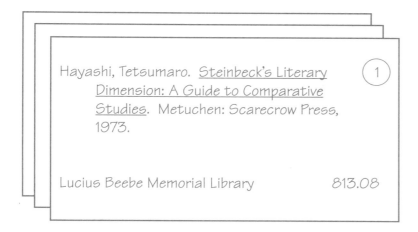

Hayashi, Tetsumaro. <u>Steinbeck's Literary Dimension: A Guide to Comparative Studies</u>. Metuchen: Scarecrow Press, 1973.

(1)

Lucius Beebe Memorial Library   813.08

Notice that a bibliography card contains all or most of the items described below.

1. A bibliographic entry gives essential information about the source, such as its author, its title, its place and/or date of publication, and the pages (of a book or magazine) on which it was found. The first line of the bibliographic entry begins in the upper left-hand corner of the card. Subsequent lines are indented a few spaces.

2. A source note tells where the researcher found the source. The source listed above was found at the Lucius Beebe Memorial Library. The source note will help you find the source again if you need to do so.

3. A source number is written in the upper right-hand corner of the card and circled. Each time you find a new source, give it a source number, starting with source number 1. You will use this number to refer to the source on any note cards containing material from that source.

4. A card catalog number, if appropriate, should be included. Books and some other materials in libraries are

Research Tip

Arts and Humanities

When doing a paper on an artist or a work of art, don't forget that works of art are themselves your primary sources. Before reading what critics have to say, spend a lot of time with the work of art and take notes on your own reactions to it.

assigned card catalog numbers. If your source comes from a library and has a card catalog number, you should write that number in the lower right-hand corner of the card. The card catalog number will help you to find the source again if you need to do so.

Every time you find a possible source, follow these steps:

Evaluating and Recording Sources

1. Evaluate the source.

2. Make a bibliography card for it, using a 3" × 5" index card or slip of paper.

3. Find the appropriate bibliography form in Appendix C on pages 82–90. Then write on the index card or slip of paper a complete bibliography entry for the source. Make sure you capitalize and punctuate the bibliography entry properly.

4. In the top right-hand corner of the card or slip of paper, record the source number and circle it.

5. At the bottom of the card or slip of paper, write the place where you found the source.

6. If the source has a card catalog number, record that number as well.

7. Put the card with the stack of cards that make up your Working Bibliography.

Gathering Information

After you have written a statement of controlling purpose and have prepared a Working Bibliography, you are ready to begin gathering information for your paper. Begin with the most promising sources on your Working Bibliography list—the ones that are the most general, the most authoritative, or the most accessible. Keeping your controlling purpose clearly in mind, start searching through your sources, looking for relevant information. Do not read, view, or listen to every part of every source. Concentrate on those parts that are relevant to your topic and your purpose.

Some nonprint sources, such as online encyclopedias, have indexes or special search features that will help you to find just those items of information that you need. If you conduct interviews as part of your research, you will be able to prepare questions beforehand to ensure that much of the information that you receive will be related to your topic and purpose.

Preparing Note Cards

There are three basic types of notes:

- A **direct quotation** repeats the words of the source exactly. Quotation marks are used around the quoted material.

- A **paraphrase** repeats an idea from the source but uses different words.

- A **summary** repeats in different words and at the same time condenses an idea taken from the source. In other words, it says the same thing in fewer words.

Take notes on 4" × 6" cards. Use cards of that size to distinguish your note cards from your 3" × 5" Working Bibliography cards. Use a separate card for each note so you can order and reorder your notes later on. As a rule of thumb, try to limit each

> "Do not read, view, or listen to every part of every source. Concentrate on those parts that are relevant to your topic and your purpose."

card to one or two sentences on a single idea or subtopic. By focusing on one idea, you can more easily group and reorganize your cards later on.

When quoting, it is extremely important that you copy each letter and punctuation mark exactly. In paraphrasing or summarizing, you need to make sure that when you put the material into your own words, you do not change the source's meaning.

Page Reference. Give this reference for all written sources except articles in encyclopedias.

- From a single page—write that number after the note.

- From consecutive pages—write first and last page numbers, as follows: 1–4.

- For numbers after 99—use only last two digits of second number, as follows: 110-15.

- From nonconsecutive pages in periodicals—give number of the first page followed by a plus sign (+), as follows: 76+.

The following note card is well prepared. It is brief and deals with a single idea. The four main parts of the note card have been labeled.

Source number (Take this number from the Working Bibliography card.)

Guideline (Keep cards with similar guidelines together.)

Note (This should be a quotation, paraphrase, summary, or a combination of those types of notes)

Page reference (See instructions above.)

One Student's Process: Maika

Steinbeck's Biblical style (16)

According to critic Harold Bloom, "Frequently, the speech rhythms of Steinbeck's chosen people echo the stately rhythms of the King James Version of the Old Testament." 45

The following note card needs improvement. It presents two unrelated ideas.

Ancestry of California farm laborers/causes (27)
of the Dust Bowl

"Throughout most of the history of California, its
farm laborers were not European in ancestry. . . .
Drought on the Great Plains created a vast dust
bowl where topsoil had literally blown away." 204

This note comes from one page of one source, but it contains two ideas that are only distantly related to one another. The writer needs to place these ideas on two separate note cards.

The note card above should be split into two separate cards.

Often you may wish to add an explanatory note to a direct quotation in order to identify who said it or to provide necessary background information. Such an explanatory note can be a summary or a paraphrase. The following note, for example, contains a summary that provides a context for the quoted material.

The Joads' idealistic expectations (3)

The Joads head to California with high hopes, but
once there they discover that for them "California
is not a Promised Land but a man-blighted Eden."
195

This note begins with a summary that introduces a quotation. Many of your notes will combine quotations with summaries or paraphrases.

The chart on the next page explains when to use the various types of notes.

When to Quote, Paraphrase, or Summarize

1. **Direct quotation.** Use direct quotation when the source material is especially well-stated—that is, when it is memorable because of its succinctness, its clarity, its liveliness, its elegance of expression, or its other exceptional qualities. Also use direct quotation when the exact wording is important historically, legally, or as a matter of definition.

2. **Paraphrase.** Use paraphrase as your most common note form. Make this the form that you always use unless you have a good reason to quote your source or to summarize it.

3. **Summary.** Use summary when the source runs too long to be succinctly quoted or paraphrased.

4. **Quotation plus summary or paraphrase.** Write this kind of note when the exact words of the source are desirable but require some explanation in order to be made clear, to be properly attributed, or to be distinguished as fact or opinion.

The following guidelines will help you to improve your note-taking skills:

Effective Note Taking

1. Keep your topic, controlling purpose, and audience in mind at all times. Do not record material unrelated to your topic.

2. Make sure that summaries or paraphrases correctly reflect the meaning of the original.

Effective Note Taking (cont.)

3. Be accurate. Make sure that direct quotations are picked up word-for-word, with capitalization, spelling, grammar, and punctuation precisely as in the original. Make sure that every direct quotation begins and ends with quotation marks.

4. Double-check statistics and facts to make sure that you have them right.

5. Distinguish between fact and opinion by labeling opinions as such: Dr. Graves thinks that . . . *or* According to Grace Jackson, . . .

6. Nonessential parts of a quotation can be cut if the overall meaning of the quotation is not changed. Indicate omissions of nonessential material from a quotation by using **ellipsis points,** a series of three or four spaced dots. Use three dots (. . .) when cutting material within a single sentence. Use four dots (. . . .) when cutting a full sentence, a paragraph, or more than a paragraph from a quotation. Also use four dots when cutting material from the end of a sentence.

7. Always double-check page references. It's easy to copy these incorrectly.

Research Tip

History, Social Studies, Science, and Mathematics

Many topics in these fields involve facts and statistics. When dealing with facts and statistics:

1. Always double-check them to make sure that you are transcribing them accurately.

2. When possible, check facts and statistics in at least two different sources.

3. Use sources that are well respected and authoritative.

Avoiding Plagiarism

One of the purposes of using a Working Bibliography and note cards is to help you to avoid plagiarism. **Plagiarism** is the act of intentionally or unintentionally treating work done by someone else as though it were your own. In most schools, including high schools and universities, plagiarism is considered a serious offense and can result in severe penalties such as failing grades, loss of course credit, or even expulsion.

Given the seriousness of plagiarism, it is important to know exactly what it is and what you can do to avoid it. Here is a simple test to determine whether something is plagiarized: Ask yourself, Is this information, idea, or statement common knowledge? If the answer is no, then ask yourself, Did this information, idea, or statement come from a source outside myself, or did it come from my own experience or as a result of my own creative activity? If the information, idea, or statement is not common knowledge, and if it came from an outside source, then you must credit that source. Failure to do so constitutes plagiarism.

Developing a Preliminary Outline

At some point early in your research, you will come to know enough about your topic to begin to develop a **preliminary**, or **rough, outline**. A preliminary outline is useful because it will help you to focus your search for information. The preliminary outline should list some key ideas or subtopics that you expect to include in the body of your paper. As you learn more about your topic, your preliminary outline will change and grow, but even a short, incomplete preliminary outline can be useful.

One Student's Process: Maika

Soon after Maika began her research on *The Grapes of Wrath*, she decided that she might organize her paper by writing first about what happened in real life and then about what happened in the novel. In other words, she would start with the history and then tell Steinbeck's version of it. Rather than writing a complete outline, she started with these two main ideas:

What happened (the history)
—The Dust Bowl
—The migration to California
Steinbeck's version of it (the novel)
—The Dust Bowl
—The migration to California

> "If the information, idea, or statement is not common knowledge, and if it came from an outside source, then you must credit that source. Failure to do so constitutes plagiarism."

A preliminary outline can consist of a few heads or of many. In a preliminary outline, all heads are usually written beginning at the left-hand margin, and subheads are introduced by dashes.

The Note Taking/Outlining Cycle

Writing is a cyclical process. At any point in the process, you can stop what you are doing and return to an earlier point. For example, you might decide after doing a bit of research to return to the very beginning and to choose a new topic, or you might decide to change your statement of controlling purpose. In other words, you are free to return to the beginning and to start the writing cycle all over again.

Nowhere in the process of preparing a research paper is the cyclical nature of writing more apparent than in the stage in which you gather information. During this stage, you will continually go back and forth between your preliminary outline and your note cards. As you do more research and take more notes, you will acquire more and more information that you can use to improve your outline. As you change the headings in your outline, you will want to reorganize your note cards, to change guidelines on those note cards, and to take new notes related to your outline's headings. So, your notes and your outline will grow and change together—each one feeding into the other.

> "Your notes and your outline will grow and change together—each one feeding into the other."

5

Organizing Your Material

In the preceding chapter you learned that research is a cyclical process. The more research you do, and the more information you gather onto note cards, the more you will understand your topic. The more you understand your topic, the more detailed you can make your preliminary outline. The more detailed your preliminary outline becomes, the more you will understand what additional information you need to gather.

At first your preliminary outline will probably be sketchy. However, over time it will become quite detailed. To develop a detailed outline, you will need to consider, over and over again, how best to organize the information that you are gathering. Of course, as you write and research, the order of the outline can and probably will change.

Organizing Ideas in a Research Paper

Much of the writing that people do is fiction, how-to writing, or personal correspondence, and almost all of this writing is in chronological order. The writing that is left over, including a great deal of nonfiction, is usually organized not in any one way but in what might be called **part-by-part order.** One idea or group of ideas suggests another, which suggests another, and so on to the end. Each idea is related in some way to the one that precedes it and to the one that follows it, but no single, overall method of organization is used.

There are even more possible ways to organize research papers than there are possible topics for such papers. Consequently, there are no hard-and-fast rules about how ideas in research papers should be organized. However, here are some guidelines to keep in mind:

1. Your paper will begin with an introduction that states your thesis. It will end with a conclusion that restates your thesis

> "Writing . . . is usually organized not in any one way but in what might be called part-by-part order. One idea or group of ideas suggests another, which suggests another, and so on to the end."

and that summarizes the main point or points of the paper. You need to concentrate on organizing the body of the paper. Your goal is to find a sensible method of arranging the evidence that you will present in the body.

2. Many topics require that you start by providing background information. If you have chosen such a topic, think about what essential background information should appear early on, and group that information together. You might want to include among this background information definitions of any key terms that will appear in your paper.

3. Remember that events are usually presented in chronological order, unless there is a good reason to present them in some other way. So, if part or all of your paper involves presenting events, consider organizing those events chronologically.

4. As you gather your notes, or evidence, physically sort the notes into separate piles of related ideas and information. Try different combinations, and make rough outlines based on them.

5. Once you have your note cards separated into piles of related ideas and information, come up with a phrase to describe what is in each pile. Think about the different possible orders in which you could present each group of ideas. Should the ideas in pile one be presented first, or those in pile three? Why?

6. Look for relationships between the ideas and information in each group of note cards. Also look for relationships between groups of cards. The following chart describes some of the relationships among ideas that you might discover:

Research Tip

History, Social Studies, Science, and Mathematics

Research papers on topics in these fields often have as their major purpose explaining why something is so, why something occurred, or why something occurs. Therefore, such papers often follow cause-and-effect order, at least in part.

Ways to Relate Ideas

1. **Chronological order:** from first event to last event or last event to first

2. **Spatial order:** order of appearance in space

3. **Classification:** grouping on the basis of similar properties or characteristics

Research papers in the arts and humanities often deal with a particular style of art, such as Baroque or Expressionist or Post modern. A common method of organization is to begin with a definition of the style and then to give examples of it.

Ways to Relate Ideas (cont.)

4. **Order of degree:** order of importance, value, interest, obviousness, certainty, etc.

5. **Cause-and-effect order:** from cause to effect or effect to cause

6. **Comparison and contrast order:** similarities followed by differences or differences followed by similarities

7. **Analytical order:** description of parts and of relationships between the parts

8. **Inductive order, or synthesis:** presentation of specific examples followed by generalization from those examples

9. **Deductive order:** presentation of a general idea or principle followed by specific conclusions drawn from that general idea or principle

10. **Order of impression, or association:** the order in which things strike one's attention

11. **Hierarchical order:** from class to subclass (group within a class) or vice versa

Creating a Draft Outline

Before beginning your rough draft, you will want to create a draft outline. A **draft outline** is a formal outline that is used as the basis for a rough draft. It can be a **sentence outline,** containing entries that are all complete sentences, or it can be a **topic outline,** containing entries that are words, phrases, or clauses.

The draft outline begins with the statement of controlling purpose. It is divided into two or more major sections introduced by Roman numerals (I, II). Each major section is divided into two or more subsections introduced by capital letters (A, B).

The subsections may be divided into sub-subsections introduced by Arabic numerals (1, 2), and those into sub-sub-subsections introduced by lowercase letters (a, b).

One Student's Process: Maika

Maika wrote a draft outline for her paper on Steinbeck's *The Grapes of Wrath*. Maika chose to produce a topic outline:

Topic Outline

```
       The Political Message of John Steinbeck's
                  The Grapes of Wrath
Controlling Purpose: The purpose of this
paper is to show that Steinbeck's novel
expressed a strong political message; it
warned that exploitation of migrant workers
would cause them to rise up as a group
against their oppressors, the state and the
wealthy landowners.
    I.   The historical background of the
         migrant situation
         A. The Dust Bowl of the 1930s
         B. The migration to California
         C. The nature of California
            agriculture
         D. The living conditions among the
            migrants
   II.   Steinbeck's opinions about the migrant
         situation
         A. Steinbeck's publication of Their
            Blood Is Strong
         B. Steinbeck's descriptions of the
            migrants' lives
         C. Steinbeck's warning about the
            consequences of exploitation
  III.   Steinbeck's message about the migrant
         situation in The Grapes of Wrath
```

When preparing a formal outline for submission to a teacher or to a peer reviewer, always double-space the outline. On the first page of the outline, include your name, teacher's name, class, and the date, as shown on the sample research paper on page 5 of this book. Then, on subsequent pages, if there are any, give your last name and the page number in the upper right-hand corner.

    A. The Joads as self-absorbed, passive victims
    B. The Joads as active agents of change
    C. The conclusion of the novel as a warning
    D. The title of the novel as a parallel between the migrant system and Babylon

Here is how the last section would look if this were a sentence outline:

III.   What was Steinbeck's message about the migrant situation in <u>The Grapes of Wrath</u>?
    A. The Joads began their time of struggle as self-absorbed, passive victims.
    B. During the struggle, the Joads became active agents of change.
    C. The conclusion of the novel is a warning.
    D. The title of the novel shows a parallel between the migrant system and Babylon.

Drafting Your Research Paper

After completing a draft outline and placing your note cards in the order of that outline, you are ready to begin writing your rough draft. The comforting thing about a rough draft is that it does not have to be perfect. You can rework your draft as often as you like and watch it take shape gradually. In other words, you do not have to hit a home run your first time at bat. You can have as many chances at the plate as you want.

Approaches to Drafting

With regard to drafting, writers fall into two major camps. Some prefer to get everything down on paper quickly but in very rough form and then to do one or more detailed revisions. Others like to complete each section as they go, writing and polishing one section, then moving on to the next. Either approach is acceptable. If you choose the second approach, however, you might want to look first at pages 57–62, on revision.

The Style of the Draft

A research paper is a type of objective, formal writing. Therefore, you should avoid making the paper personal and subjective, and you should avoid using informal language. Do not use such words as *I, me, my, mine, we,* and *our.* Do not state opinions without supporting them with facts. Do not use slang, colloquialisms, nonstandard dialect, or contractions. Avoid referring to your paper except when summarizing its contents.

Assembling the Draft

A rough draft is just that—it is rough, or unfinished. As you draft, do not worry about matters that you can take care of later,

> "You do not have to hit a home run your first time at bat. You can have as many chances at the plate as you want."

such as the details of spelling, grammar, usage, or mechanics. Instead, concentrate on getting your ideas down in an order that makes sense.

Use your outline as a guide. Explore each main point, supporting the idea with evidence from your note cards. When you use information from a note card, write the source number from the note card on your draft and circle it. Noting the source number is extremely important because during revision you will have to find the source in order to document it.

"Use your outline as a guide. Explore each main point, supporting the idea with evidence from your note cards.**"**

One Student's Process: Maika

One of the major heads in Maika's outline for her paper on John Steinbeck was the following:

```
What was the migration to
California?
```

Maika turned this head into a statement, which she used as a topic sentence:

```
The Dust Bowl led to a massive
migration, or movement, of people from
Oklahoma to California.
```

Then she added material from her note cards to support the topic sentence:

```
The Dust Bowl led to a massive
migration. People went from Oklahoma to
California--300,000 to 400,000 homeless
farmers from the Dust Bowl area packed
everything into old cars or trucks and
headed to California to find work. The
panhandle region lost more than half its
residents (16). But when they got to
California, they did not find paradise.
They found "not a Promised Land but a
man-blighted Eden" (4).
```

Notice that Maika added both paraphrased and quoted material. In each case she has included a source number from her note card so that she will be able to find that source later on, when she is preparing the documentation, or full source information, for her paper.

Incorporating summaries and paraphrases. Working summaries and paraphrases into your paper is quite easy. Simply write them out as part of your text and include a source number at the end of the summarized or paraphrased material. Just be certain that transitions connect the material smoothly to whatever precedes or follows it.

Incorporating quotations. Working quotations into your paper is a bit more complicated because there are many ways in which quotations can be used. The rules also differ for prose on the one hand and poetry or song lyrics on the other. See the chart on pages 50–51 for complete instructions on using quotations in your draft.

The Draft as a Work in Progress

Occasionally, as you write, you may discover gaps in the information that you have gathered. In other words, you may find that you do not have in your note cards all the information you need to make some point. When that occurs, you can stop and look for the information, or you can simply make a note to yourself to find the information later on. Either approach is acceptable.

The need to fill gaps is one example of a general characteristic of drafting: that drafting is still discovery time. In addition to discovering gaps to be filled, you may discover better ways to organize parts of the paper, contradictions in your source materials, or significant parts of your topic that you have not yet explored. You may even find a whole new approach to your topic that would be more interesting or workable than the one you have taken. Remain open to these developments—to the discoveries that occur as you draft. Be willing to return to previous stages of the writing process, if necessary, to do more research, to revise your controlling purpose, or to change your outline.

"Drafting is still discovery time."

49

Quoting Prose Works

1. If the quotation is four lines long or less, put it in quotation marks and place it in the text of your paper:

   ```
   An actress who visited one of the migrant camps wrote,
   "I went around in a sick daze for hours after witness-
   ing unimaginable suffering" (13) .
   ```

   Of course, the circled number is the source number from your Working Bibliography card. When you do your final documentation, this number will be replaced with a citation in parentheses. (See pages 63–70.)

2. You do not have to quote complete sentences:

   ```
   An actress who visited one of the migrant camps wrote
   of seeing "unimaginable suffering" (13) .
   ```

3. You can also break a quotation in two:

   ```
   "I went around in a sick daze for hours," said an
   actress who visited the camps, "after witnessing
   unimaginable suffering" (13) .
   ```

4. When a quoted passage runs to more than four lines, set it off from the text of your paper. Put a colon after the statement that immediately precedes the quotation. Begin a new line. Indent the entire quotation ten spaces from the left-hand margin. Double-space the quotation and leave out the quotation marks:

   ```
       The extent of the desperation was made clear in a
   report written in 1939, the year that The Grapes of
   Wrath was published:
               The State Relief Administration estimates
               that most agricultural workers only have
               employment for six months in the year or
               less; and that the average yearly earnings
               per family . . . [were] $289 in 1935 (17) .
   ```

5. When quoting more than one paragraph, indent the first line of each full paragraph an additional three spaces. However, indent the first sentence only if it begins a paragraph in your source.

Quoting Prose Works (cont.)

```
The migrants also faced an even more terrible problem:
        There has been no war in California, no
        plague, no bombing of open towns and roads,
        no shelling of cities.  It is a beautiful
        year.  And thousands of families are
        starving. . . .
            [It's] in the tents you see along the
        roads and in the shacks built from dump heap
        materials that the hunger is, and it isn't
        malnutrition.  It is starvation. (19)
```

Quoting Poetry, Verse Plays, and Songs

1. When quoting a single line or part of a line, simply place the material in your text with quotation marks around it:

```
Shakespeare's Macbeth says: "Life's but a walking
shadow"( 4 ).
```

2. When quoting two or three lines, separate the lines with a space, a slash (/), and another space:

```
Shakespeare's Macbeth says: "Life's but a walking
shadow, a poor player, / That struts and frets his hour
upon the stage / And then is heard no more"( 4 ).
```

3. When quoting four or more lines, set the material off from your text. Indent it ten spaces, double-space, and do not add quotation marks. Follow the line division and spacing of the original:

```
Shakespeare's Macbeth says:
        Life's but a walking shadow, a poor player,
        That struts and frets his hour upon the stage
        And then is heard no more.  It is a tale
        Told by an idiot, full of sound and fury,
        Signifying nothing.( 4 )
```

Using Graphic Aids

As you draft, stay alert to the possibility of using tables, maps, charts, diagrams, and other **graphic aids** to present information concisely. If you use a graphic aid from a source, or if you use information from a source to create a graphic aid, then you must credit the source of the information.

Tables, Maps, Graphs, Illustrations, and Other Graphic Aids. Tables should be labeled Table 1, Table 2, and so on. Other graphic aids should be labeled Figure 1, Figure 2, and so on. Place the label after the figure and follow it with a caption that is either the title of the graphic aid or that describes the graphic aid. Follow that with a source note entry in endnote form of the kind used for tables.

One Student's Process: Marcus

Marcus was doing a paper on the attack of the African-American Massachusetts 54th Infantry regiment on the Confederate stronghold of Fort Wagner, South Carolina, during the Civil War. His completed paper is on pages 104 – 10. Here is a graphic that Marcus created based on a map that he found while doing his research:

Figure 1. Charleston harbor, 1863. Adapted from: Peter Burchard, <u>One Gallant Rush: Robert Gould Shaw and His Brave Black Regiment</u> (New York: St. Martin's, 1965) 110.

Charleston

Battery Wagner

N

ATLANTIC OCEAN

Charleston Harbor in 1863

Writing the Introduction

The introduction to a research paper should accomplish two purposes:

1. It should grab the reader's attention.

2. It should present the paper's main idea, or **thesis statement.**

In addition, the introduction may define key terms, supply necessary background information, or both. The introduction can be of any length, although most introductions are one or two paragraphs long.

Capturing the Reader's Attention

There are many ways to capture a reader's attention in an introduction. You can begin with a startling or unusual fact, with a question, with an anecdote (a brief story that makes a point), with an analogy (a comparison between the topic and something with which the reader is already familiar), with a paragraph that compares or contrasts, or with examples.

Writing the Thesis Statement

To create the thesis statement, you can simply recast your statement of controlling purpose. You may decide to change the statement, however, to reflect any additional refining or refocusing of your topic that has occurred during research. In either case, avoid using the phrase "the purpose of this paper" in your final thesis statement. Notice how that phrase is eliminated in the following example.

> Statement of Controlling Purpose: The purpose of this paper is to show that Steinbeck's novel expressed a strong political message; it warned that exploitation of migrant workers would cause them to rise up as a group against their oppressors, the state and the wealthy landowners.

> "The introduction to a research paper should . . . grab the reader's attention [and] . . . present the paper's main idea, or thesis statement."

53

Thesis Statement: Steinbeck's The Grapes
of Wrath warned that exploitation of
migrant workers would cause them to rise
up as a group against their oppressors,
the state and the wealthy landowners. But
beyond that, the novel shows how such an
oppressive situation can result in a
profound philosophical change in the
people who experience it.

Providing Background Information. Sometimes, in order for your readers to understand your thesis statement, you will have to provide some additional background information. In an introduction you need provide only enough information to make it possible for them to understand the thesis statement. You can provide additional information, as necessary, in the body of your paper.

One Student's Process: Marcus

Marcus's thesis statement for his paper on the Massachusetts 54th Infantry Regiment was, "Although many Yankee soldiers lost their lives in the charge on Fort Wagner, and although the Confederates technically won the battle, the charge of the Massachusetts 54th was a great victory for the North and for the antislavery movement." Since some readers might never have heard of the Massachusetts 54th or of Fort Wagner, Marcus decided to open with some background information:

On July 18, 1863, at the height of the
Civil War, the men of the African-American
54th Massachusetts infantry attacked a South
Carolina earthwork known as Fort Wagner or
Battery Wagner. When the fighting was done,
nearly half of those men lay dead in what
was by all accounts a massacre, an

overwhelming victory for the Confederacy ⑧.
However, the African-American soldiers of
the 54th had fought as free men. So
although many of these Yankee soldiers lost
their lives in the charge, and although the
Confederates technically won the battle, the
charge of the Massachusetts 54th was a
moral, if not a military, victory for the
North and for the antislavery movement.

One Student's Process: Maika

In her introduction, Maika wanted to accomplish two
purposes: she wanted to introduce the concept of the
political novel, and she wanted to state her thesis, or
main idea. She decided to begin with a comparison and
some examples that clarify what a political novel is:

A novel, like a movie, is a form of
entertainment. However, some novels do a
great deal more than entertain. Some pack a
powerful political message. For example,
Uncle Tom's Cabin, by Harriet Beecher Stowe,
created controversy from the moment it was
published. The Jungle, by Upton Sinclair,
alerted the country to the horrors of the
meatpacking industry.

Then, in the last two sentences of her second paragraph,
Maika introduced her thesis statement.

John Steinbeck's The Grapes of Wrath is
another example of a novel with a powerful
political message. It warned that
exploitation of migrant workers would cause

```
them to rise up as a group against their
oppressors, the state and the wealthy
landowners.  Beyond that, the novel showed
how such an oppressive situation can result
in a profound philosophical change in the
people who experience it.  Steinbeck
demonstrated this by showing how one migrant
family becomes politicized.
```

Writing the Conclusion

Like the introduction, the conclusion is usually one or two paragraphs long. The most common way to conclude a research paper is to restate the main idea and the principal arguments presented to support that idea. In addition, you may wish to use the conclusion to tie up any loose ends left by the body of your paper, to explain consequences of accepting the truth of the thesis statement, to call on the reader to take some action, to explain the importance or value of what the reader has learned from the paper, or to make projections about the future. The conclusion is an opportunity to be imaginative. Almost anything is acceptable as long as the reader is left with a satisfactory sense that the treatment of the subject has been completed. (See the sample conclusions on pages 17 and 108 of this book.)

> “ The conclusion is an opportunity to be imaginative. Almost anything is acceptable as long as the reader is left with a satisfactory sense that the treatment of the subject has been completed. ”

7

Revising Your Research Paper

After you finish drafting your research paper, put it aside for a day or so. Distancing yourself from the paper will help you to view it more objectively in preparation for revising it.

Expect the revision of your paper to take place over several days, and expect to revise your paper more than once. One excellent approach is to do separate revisions for content and organization, for style, and for documentation. During revision, do not worry about the details of spelling, grammar, usage, and mechanics. You can clean up problems in those areas later on, during the proofreading stage. With regard to documentation, all you have to worry about at this point is having a source number in your manuscript for every instance where you have used a source. The next chapter will explain how to turn the source numbers into complete, final documentation for your paper.

Peer Response

At some point during the drafting process, give your paper to one of your peers, or fellow students, for review. By having a peer review your paper, you can find out whether you've fulfilled your purpose, whether you have been completely clear, what parts cause problems for readers, and so on.

Do not worry about losing control of your work. You maintain the right to accept or reject any suggestions that your peer reviewer makes. Here are some questions you can ask your peer reviewer to elicit useful responses from him or her:

Questions for Peer Readers

- What do you think my main point, or thesis, is? Do you think I have proved that point? Why, or why not? What could I do to make the proof more complete?

- Which sections of the paper did you find most interesting or informative?

- Were any parts of the paper unclear to you?

- What questions do you have about my topic now that you have read my paper? Were any important topic-related questions left unanswered?

Self-evaluation

A peer reviewer's comments can give you important insights into how a paper can be improved. However, it is also important that you conduct your own close evaluation of the paper. Ask yourself the questions on the following checklist:

Revision Checklist

CONTENT AND ORGANIZATION

General

☐ **1.** Does your paper adequately support or prove the thesis statement?

☐ **2.** Does your paper have a clear introduction, body, and conclusion?

☐ **3.** Does every idea follow logically from the one that precedes it?

☐ **4.** Have you used transitions throughout to show the connections between ideas?

Introduction

☐ **5.** Will the introduction capture your readers' attention?

☐ **6.** Does the introduction present your thesis statement clearly?

Body

☐ **7.** Does the body of your paper present evidence from a wide variety of reliable sources?

☐ **8.** Are materials from your sources presented in a combination of summary, paraphrase, and quotation?

☐ **9.** Are there any gaps in your argument that should be filled by doing additional research? Are there any points that are inadequately supported?

☐ **10.** Have all unnecessary or irrelevant materials been deleted from the body of your paper?

☐ **11.** Have you avoided unsubstantiated statements of opinion throughout?

Conclusion

☐ **12.** Did you restate your thesis in the conclusion of your paper?

☐ **13.** Does your conclusion summarize the main points that you have presented in support of the thesis?

☐ **14.** Does your conclusion give your readers a satisfactory sense of completion? (Are all the loose ends tied up? Have all the parts of the thesis been supported? Have all the readers' most likely questions about the topic been addressed?)

STYLE

☐ **15.** Have you achieved variety by using many different kinds of sentences, including short and long sentences; simple, compound, complex, and compound-complex sentences; declarative, exclamatory, and interrogative sentences; and sentences that begin with different parts of speech?

☐ **16.** Have you avoided wordiness? Have you deleted unnecessary words, phrases, or clauses?

☐ **17.** Have you used clear, concrete examples? Have you defined key terms?

☐ **18.** Have you avoided colloquial language, slang, jargon, and dialect? Have you avoided contractions, personal references, and first-person pronouns such as *I, we, me,* and *our* throughout?

☐ **19.** Are the sentences in the paper graceful and not awkward?

DOCUMENTATION

☐ **20.** Have you avoided plagiarism by completely documenting all materials taken from sources? Does every summary, paraphrase, or quotation have a corresponding source number?

☐ **21.** Is each of your direct quotations set off by quotation marks or by indention? Is each quotation accurate? Does it reflect precisely what was in the source from which it was taken?

☐ **22.** Is there a complete bibliography card, in proper form, for every source number in the final version of your manuscript? (For information on proper bibliography form, see pages 82–90.)

One Student's Process: Maika

Maika wrote a rough draft of her paper on John Steinbeck's *The Grapes of Wrath*. Then she revised the draft for content and organization. In one paragraph, she added additional information to support her opening statement and to clarify the meaning of the term *Dust Bowl*. She replaced the pronoun *he* with a proper noun to make clear whom she was writing about. She moved a sentence to improve the paragraph's organization, and she cut a sentence that was irrelevant to her topic.

_∧ a summation of national experience at a given time. Therefore,

The Grapes of Wrath is an historical novel _∧

we should recognize that it is important to

understand the historical events on which the

novel was based, ~~before one can understand the~~

~~novel.~~ The historical and economic experience

Steinbeck   that of

that ~~he~~ was reacting to was _∧ the migrents who left

Storms blew away topsoil ⑩ covered

pastures and suffocated livestock ㉓

the Oklahoma Dust Bowl in the late 1930s ⑫ . _∧

added to already low crop prices,

Crop failure led to the foreclosure of many small

farms and the homelessness of many farm families"

④ . At that time the country was in the middle of

which had reduced the prices

farmers could charge for crops

a bad period called the great depression. ~~Many~~

~~businesses in the East also closed during the~~

~~Depression.~~

One Student's Process: Maika

Then Maika revised her paragraph for style. She deleted unnecessary words, removed first-person pronouns, reordered a sentence to make it less awkward, and replaced the vague term *bad period* with a concrete, specific phrase.

Finally, Maika fixed any remaining problems in her documentation. She added a missing source number and some missing quotation marks, and she fixed a sentence that she had quoted inaccurately, adding a word that she had accidentally dropped. When she proofreads the final version of her paper, Maika will correct the remaining errors in spelling, grammar, and mechanics. Compare the revised paragraph on the preceding page to Maika's final version on pages 5–6 of this book.

Preparing a Final Outline

Your teacher may ask you to submit a final outline along with the final draft of your paper. If so, revise the last version of your draft outline, making sure to follow the guidelines for outlining given on pages 44–46. In most cases either a topic outline or a sentence outline is acceptable, though your teacher may prefer one type of outline over the other. The final outline should be typed or prepared on a word processor. For information on proper manuscript form for the outline and for the rest of the paper, see pages 74–75 of this book.

Documenting Your Sources

8

Each time you use information from your note cards, write down a source number. After you revise your draft, use the source numbers in the revised draft to prepare your documentation. **Documentation** is the information in the paper that tells what sources you used.

Parenthetical Documentation

The method of documentation most widely used today is called **parenthetical documentation**. This method has largely replaced documentation using endnotes or footnotes. (For information on endnotes, footnotes, and other alternative methods of documentation, see Appendix D, "Alternative Documentation Styles," on pages 91–111.)

To acknowledge a source using the parenthetical documentation method, enclose a brief note in parentheses. The note, which is called a **parenthetical citation**, usually consists of an author's name and a page number:

> The Grapes of Wrath is an historical novel, "a
> summation of national experience at a given
> time" (Levant 93).

The process of placing the citation into your text is called **citing a source.**

A parenthetical citation contains just enough information to help the reader locate the source in the list of **Works Cited** at the end of the paper. The list of Works Cited consists of bibliography entries like those in Appendix C on pages 82–90.

Take a moment to look at the sample research paper on pages 5–19. Study the examples of parenthetical documentation throughout the paper. Then look at the list of Works Cited on pages 18–19, at the end of the sample paper.

Preparing Parenthetical Citations

Preparing parenthetical citations to document your sources is fairly straightforward, and by creating them you make your sources easily accessible to your reader. The following guidelines will help you to cite your sources properly:

1. Basic citation. Place the citation at the end of the sentence that contains the material being documented. The citation should appear after the text of the sentence but before the end mark.

```
The Oklahoma migrants found "not a Promised
Land but a man-blighted Eden" (Crockett 195).
```

2. Citation of a long quotation. When documenting a long quotation that is set off from the text, place the citation after the end punctuation. Space twice before the citation.

```
No one is really certain about the origins
of the term "Dust Bowl":
          H. L. Mencken in a footnote to the
          first supplement (1945) to his
          monumental The American Language
          traces the term . . . to an
          Associated Press dispatch sent by
          staff writer Robert Geiger from
          Guymon, Oklahoma, on April 15, 1935.
          (French, Companion 3)
```

3. Basic citation with author's name in text. If the name of the author is clear from the context in which the parenthetical reference appears, then give only the page number.

```
As critic H. Kelly Crockett has pointed
out, the Oklahoma migrants found "not a
Promised Land but a man-blighted Eden" (195).
```

4. Citation of multiple works by one author. If the list of Works Cited contains more than one work by the author, then include an abbreviated version of the title. When abbreviating a title, drop small opening words like *a, an,* or *the;* begin with the word that the full title would be alphabetized by; and reduce the overall length to one to four words. So, for example, the title <u>A Companion to</u> The Grapes of Wrath might become <u>Companion</u>.

> The success of <u>The Grapes of Wrath</u> overshadowed
>
> Steinbeck's later work (French, <u>Companion</u> ix).

5. Citation with author's name and title in text. If the name of the author and the title of the work both appear in the text of your paper, use only the page number, even if more than one work by the author is listed in your list of Works Cited.

> In "The Commonplace and the Grotesque," critic
>
> Edwin Bowdin points out that Steinbeck's novel
>
> contains people who are "isolated and lonely
>
> and even grotesque" (16).

6. Citation of a work available in various editions. When citing a literary work commonly available in different editions, include information that will allow the reader to find the quotation in any edition. For novels, include chapter numbers.

> One character in Steinbeck's novel points out
>
> that "Everybody says words different. . . .
>
> Arkansas folks says 'em different, and Oklahomy
>
> folks says 'em different. And we seen a lady
>
> from Massachusetts, an' she said 'em
>
> differentest of all" (<u>Grapes</u> 173; ch. 13).

For short stories or essays, include paragraph numbers: (Donne, "Meditation 17" 300; par. 7). For plays divided into acts and scenes, give the act number and the scene number separated by a period. Omit the page number(s). If the play is a well-known classic, then the author's name can be omitted as well: (<u>Macbeth</u> 5.5).

7. Citation of an anonymous work. When citing an anonymous work (one for which no author is given), give an abbreviated, or shortened, version of the title, followed by the page number. Make sure that the first word in your abbreviated version of the title is the word by which the work is alphabetized in the list of Works Cited. Here is a citation for an anonymous work called "Some Factual Errors in Steinbeck's Portrayal of Oklahoma and Oklahomans":

```
One contributor wrote that the novel contained
"a number of factual errors" ("Some Errors"
647).
```

8. Citation of an encyclopedia or a similar reference work. When citing an article in a reference work that is arranged alphabetically—an article in an encyclopedia or in a biographical dictionary, for example—give only the title or a shortened version of the title.

```
One cause of the Dust Bowl was misuse of the
land ("Dust Bowl").
```

9. Citation of a work by two or three authors. When citing a work by two or three authors, give the authors' last names and the page number.

```
Very little is now known about how dolphins and
whales communicate (Akmajian, Demers, and
Harnish 36).
```

10. Citation of a work by more than three authors. When citing a work by more than three authors, give the last name of the first author, followed by *et al.* and the page number. *Et* is the Latin word for "and." *Al.* is an abbreviation for the Latin word *alii,* meaning "others."

```
Scientists are still debating whether the
higher apes can be taught to create "sentences"
in sign language (Kim et al. 427).
```

11. Citation of a quotation appearing in a source.
When citing a source that is quoted by your source, use the abbreviation *qtd. in:*

> An actress who visited one of these camps
>
> wrote, "I went around in a sick daze for hours
>
> after witnessing unimaginable suffering" (qtd.
>
> in Stein 219).

12. Citation of a nonpaginated source. If the source is something that does not have page numbers, an interview, a piece of computer software, or a recording, for example, give the name of the author or interviewee. If there is no name, give a title or a shortened version of the title.

> The migrants didn't have the necessary money,
>
> or "Do-Re-Me," to live decently (Guthrie).

13. Citation of a multivolume work. To cite a page number in a multivolume work that is *not* an alphabetically organized reference work, give the name, the volume number, a colon, and the page reference.

> Today, specialists in language often use the
>
> term <u>grammar</u> to refer to any aspect of language
>
> that can be described systematically (Lyons
>
> 2:378).

14. Citation of more than one page. When citing more than one page, use a hyphen to separate the numbers unless the pages are nonconsecutive.

> French points out that "<u>The Grapes of Wrath</u> has
>
> been applauded throughout the world since its
>
> publication" (<u>Companion</u> 147-48).

When citing numbers, give the complete form of the second number for numbers through 99: 1–2, 13–15, 35–36, 67–69. When citing larger numbers, give only the last two digits of the second number unless more numbers are required for clarity's sake: 99–102, 117–18, 223–24, 1201–02, 1201–303.

Preparing the List of Works Cited

Each time you cite a source in your paper, pull the bibliography card for that source from your stack of bibliography cards and place it into a new stack of Works Cited cards. When you have completed writing all the parenthetical citations for your paper, you will have a complete set of Works Cited cards. Put those cards into alphabetical order. Then type up your final list of Works Cited from the cards, following their style exactly. Your final Works Cited should give complete bibliography entries for all the sources that you have cited in your paper. Here is a sample list of Works Cited for a research paper on saving forests:

Pappas 23

Works Cited

Caldicott, Helen. <u>If You Love This Planet: A Plan to Heal the Earth</u>. New York: Norton, 1992.

Czapski, Silvia. "Grassroots Environmentalism in Brazil." <u>The Conservationist</u> July-Aug. 1991: 42-47.

Dietrich, William. <u>The Final Forest: The Battle for the Last Great Trees of the Pacific Northwest</u>. New York: Simon, 1992.

Frome, Michael. <u>Regreening the National Parks</u>. Tucson: U of Arizona P, 1992.

Hamilton, Harriet. "From Stones and Clay an Abundance of Trees." <u>The Conservationist</u> Sep.-Oct. 1991: 32-35.

Harrison, Robert Pogue. <u>Forests: The</u>

<u>Shadow of Civilization</u>. Chicago: U of

Chicago P, 1992.

Kahak, E. "Perceiving the Good." <u>The</u>

<u>Wilderness Condition: Essays on</u>

<u>Environment and Civilization</u>. Ed. Max

Oelschaeger. San Francisco: Sierra

Club, 1992. 173-87.

Kernan, Henry S. "The World Is My Woodlot

Too." <u>The Conservationist</u> Jan.-Feb.

1992: 44-47.

Ketchledge, Edwin H. "Born-Again Forest."

<u>Natural History</u> May 1992: 34-38.

Snyder, Gary. "Etiquette of Freedom."

<u>The Wilderness Condition: Essays on</u>

<u>Environment and Civilization</u>. Ed. Max

Oelschaeger. San Francisco: Sierra

Club, 1992. 21-39.

> " Your final
> Works Cited should
> give complete
> bibliography entries
> for all the sources
> that you have cited
> in your paper. "

If you use more than one work by the same author, put them in alphabetical order. Give the author's name for the first work. Thereafter, use three hyphens in place of the name.

Steinbeck, John. <u>The Grapes of Wrath</u>.

1939. New York: Penguin, 1976.

---. <u>Their Blood Is Strong</u>. San

Francisco: Lubin, 1938. Rpt. in

French, <u>Companion</u> 53-92.

If you use several pieces taken from a single work, you can give one complete bibliography entry for that work without listing the individual essays or articles.

Manuscript Form for the List of Works Cited

1. Begin on a new page.

2. Indent one inch from both side margins.

3. Give your last name and the page number, flush right, half an inch from the top of the paper.

4. Drop down another one-half inch and center the title Works Cited. Do not underscore or use all capital letters.

5. Double-space between each entry. Double-space between the title and the first entry.

6. Begin each entry at the left margin. Double-space each entry. Indent run-over lines five spaces from the left margin.

7. If you wish, you can break down your list of Works Cited into categories such as Books, Periodicals, and so on. If you do this, list the materials under each heading alphabetically.

Completing Your Research Paper

9

After you have finished your documentation, you are ready to proofread your paper and to prepare your final manuscript. **Proofreading** is the process of checking your paper for errors in spelling, grammar, usage, level of language, capitalization, punctuation, and documentation. The **final manuscript** is the copy of your paper that will be read by your teacher and by others.

Proofreading Your Paper

The first step after revising your paper and preparing your documentation is proofreading it to eliminate errors. When you proofread, you use symbols like those shown on page 76. The following guidelines are particularly important to keep in mind when proofreading a research paper:

Proofreading a Research Paper

1. Double-check the spellings of proper names, such as the names of people and places.

2. Check to see that any quotations that you have used fit grammatically into the sentences in which they appear.

   Ungrammatical: In the 1930s the migrants truly did "harvesting the grapes of wrath."

   Grammatical: In the 1930s the migrants truly were "harvesting the grapes of wrath."

Proofreading a Research Paper (cont.)

3. Check to see that your language is appropriately formal.

4. Check all titles to make sure that these rules have been followed:

   All titles used in the paper should appear in uppercase and lowercase letters. Titles should not be given in all capital letters.

   The following types of words, when appearing in titles, should begin with uppercase letters: adjectives, adverbs, gerunds, interjections, nouns, participles, pronouns, subordinating conjunctions, verbs, words that begin or end the title, and words that follow colons.

5. Check every sentence to make sure that it has an end mark. If the sentence contains a parenthetical citation, make sure that the citation appears before the end mark, except in the case of a long, indented quotation, which ends with an end mark followed by the parenthetical citation.

6. Check every quotation in the body of the text to make sure that it begins and ends with a quotation mark. Make sure that quotations within quotations in the body of the text are enclosed with apostrophes. If the quotation runs to more than four lines, make sure that it is set off from the body of the text, without quotation marks.

7. Check all titles to make sure that they are punctuated properly.

8. Check to see that ellipsis points have been used properly in edited quotations. (See page 39.)

Proofreading a Research Paper (cont.)

9. Make sure that every quotation, summary, or paraphrase is followed by a parenthetical citation. Make sure that every citation corresponds to an entry in the list of Works Cited.

10. Check every quotation against your note cards to make sure that it is accurate.

Preparing the Final Manuscript

After proofreading you need to prepare your final manuscript. The chart on the next two pages describes a recommended manuscript form for research papers. You may also wish to refer to the sample research paper on pages 5–19.

After preparing the final manuscript, proofread it one last time. Mark any corrections neatly on the manuscript using the proofreading symbols given in the chart on page 76. If a page contains more than three proofreading corrections, consider creating a new final page.

Finally, get together all the pieces that your teacher wishes to see—your paper, your list of Works Cited, and, if requested, your final outline, your note cards, and your bibliography cards. Congratulations! You have just finished your research paper.

Reflecting on the Process

Do some thinking about your experience writing this paper while it is still fresh in your mind. If you reflect now, you may gather some tips that will save you time later as you work on your next research paper. In your jounral, write about your research experience. Consider questions such as, What have I learned? What parts of the research process were easiest or most difficult for me? What would I do differently next time?

Guidelines for Manuscript Form: Research Papers

1. **General guidelines/type of paper.** If possible, type or word process your paper. Use high-quality white, unlined 8 1/2" × 11" paper. Do not use colored paper, transparent paper, onionskin paper, or odd typefaces such as script. For information on using word processors with research papers, see Appendix A on pages 77–78.

   If you must write your paper out by hand, print or use cursive writing, whichever is neater. Use lined paper, write on only one side of the paper, and follow the same guidelines for format that you would follow when typing or word processing.

2. **Margins.** Use one-inch margins at the top, sides, and bottom.

3. **Name and page numbers.** Place your last name, a space, and the page number at the top of each page of the paper, flush with the right-hand margin. The name and page number should appear one-half-inch from the top edge of the paper. Number the paper and the list of Works Cited continuously, using Arabic numerals (1, 2, 3, and so on). Do not precede the number with the word *page* or any abbreviation such as *p., pp.,* or *pg.*

4. **Spacing.** Double-space the entire paper, including headings, titles, quotations, and text paragraphs.

5. **Heading.** On the first page, drop down one inch from the top edge of the paper and give, at the left-hand margin and on separate lines, your complete name, your teacher's name, the name of your class, and the complete date in this form: 12 November 1994. Double-space between the lines.

6. **Title.** On the line following the date, center the title of your paper. Use upper and lowercase letters, not all caps, and underline only those words, such as the titles of long works, that you would underline in the body of your paper. Double-space between the date and the title and between the title and the first paragraph of the paper.

Guidelines for Manuscript Form: Research Papers (cont.)

7. **Indentions.** Indent paragraphs in your paper five spaces from the left margin.

8. **Quotations.** See the guidelines for using quotations on pages 50–51.

9. **Paragraphing.** Do not leave a single line of a paragraph at the bottom of a page.

10. **Works Cited.** On the Works Cited page, after your last name and the page number, drop down an additional one-half inch to a position one inch from the top edge of the paper and center the title Works Cited. Do not underline the title or place it in quotation marks.

11. **Placement and spacing of Works Cited entries.** Double-space after the title Works Cited and begin the first Works Cited entry.

    Double-space and alphabetize all the Works Cited entries. Entries should be alphabetized by the first word in each entry, whether that word is a title or a person's name. If the entry is a title, skip any initial articles (*a, an,* or *the*) when alphabetizing.

    Begin the first line of each Works Cited entry flush left. Indent subsequent lines five spaces from the left margin.

12. **Binding and presentation.** Do not staple your research paper, and do not use rubber bands. Follow the instructions for binding and presentation given by your teacher. Most teachers will simply ask that you fasten the pages together with a paper clip.

13. **Final outline.** If your teacher asks you to submit a final outline along with your research paper, refer to the sample outlines on pages 45–46. Note that your final outline will differ from the sample outlines only in that the statement of controlling purpose will be replaced by your thesis statement. When preparing the final outline, follow the format of the sample outlines on pages 45–46.

Proofreading Symbols

North of Mexico	Make lowercase.
President jefferson	Capitalize.
a fine thing idea	Replace.
this this time	Delete.
thiet	Transpose.
1, 2 or 3	Add a comma.
Lets go.	Add an apostrophe.
Welcome, friends	Add a period.
are They leaving.	Add letters or words.

Computers and the Research Paper

The widespread availability and use of personal computers has changed the ways in which many people do research papers. Computers are tools that extend human capabilities and ease repetitive or time-consuming tasks. If you have access to a personal computer at home or at school, consider using it to prepare your research paper. The following are some suggestions about how personal computers can be used in the various stages of the research process.

1. **Finding sources.** Many libraries have computerized card catalogs that can help you to find sources. You can also use a personal computer to find information directly (see notes 2 and 3 below).

2. **Using online services.** Of particular value as sources of information are online computer information services. These services offer current facts and news; online encyclopedias; access to abstracts or to full versions of periodicals, reports, and government documents; homework assistance; tutoring; classes in particular subjects; and research assistance. A few of the online services offer connections to institutions such as libraries and museums, including the Library of Congress and the Smithsonian Institution in Washington, DC. To use an online computer information service, you need a personal computer, a modem, and communications software. A local computer dealer or computer users' group will probably be able to help you choose an information service that is right for your needs.

3. **Using computer networks.** Some local school districts and some states have special education networks to connect students, teachers, and administrators. An example of such a network is the TENET, or Texas Education Network, which is itself connected to the INTERNET, a massive computer network that connects businesses, universities, and government research centers around the globe. Check with your teacher to see if your school is connected to such a

network and to see if the network is available for use by students at your school.

4. **Using CD-ROM.** If you have access to a CD-ROM drive, you will be able to use some of the many resource materials—from timetables of history or science to encyclopedias to the works of Shakespeare—that are available on CD-ROM disks. Again, see your local computer dealer about purchasing such disks, or see if your school or community library has a CD-ROM collection.

5. **Preparing computerized bibliography cards and note cards.** If you are familiar with the use of database or hypertext programs, then you know that such programs can easily be used for preparing note cards and bibliography cards. The advantage of preparing note cards and bibliography cards with such programs is that you can sort the cards automatically, in alphabetical or in numerical order, according to any element on them, such as the names of authors or editors, the guidelines, or the source numbers.

6. **Using documentation software.** Several programs are now available to generate bibliographies, lists of Works Cited, endnotes, and footnotes automatically, and some word-processing programs have built-in documentation features. However, before you use such a program, make sure that it follows the style that is specified in this book—the style described in the *MLA Handbook for Writers of Research Papers.*

7. **Using outlining software.** Many word-processing programs have built-in outlining features. Separate, stand-alone outlining programs are also available. However, be careful that any such program that you use creates outlines in the form described in this book or in a form acceptable to your teacher.

8. **Creating graphics.** Personal computers can, of course, be used to prepare graphics for use in research papers. Excellent programs exist for drawing, for creating charts and tables, for creating graphs of all kinds, and for mapping.

Abbreviations for Use in Research Papers

Dates and Geographical Names

See a dictionary or the *MLA Handbook for Writers of Research Papers* for abbreviations of days, months, and geographical names.

Publishers

In those parts of Works Cited entries, footnotes, or endnotes that give publishers' names, do not use articles (*a, an,* or *the*), abbreviations that describe business entities (*Co., Inc., Ltd.*), or words that describe the business that the publisher is in (*Books, House, Press, Publishers*). However, use the abbreviations *U* for "University" and *P* for "Press" in Works Cited entries for university press publications, as in *MIT P, U of Texas P, U of Puerto Rico P,* and *Cambridge UP.*

Use the following accepted shortened forms of publishers' names. If the publishing-house name consists of a person's name (Jeremy P. Tarcher, Inc.), then use the last name as the shortened form (Tarcher). If the publisher does not appear on the following list or if the name of the publishing house is not a person's name, consult the *MLA Handbook for Writers of Research Papers,* use an abbreviation of your own that clearly identifies the publisher, or give the publisher's name in full, except for articles, abbreviations that describe business entities, and words that describe the business that the publisher is in.

Abrams	Harry N. Abrams, Inc.	ALA	American Library Association
Allyn	Allyn and Bacon, Inc.	Appleton	Appleton-Century-Crofts
Ballantine	Ballantine Books, Inc.	Bantam	Bantam Books, Inc.
Barnes	Barnes and Noble Books	Basic	Basic Books

Bobbs	The Bobbs-Merrill Co., Inc.	Clarendon	Clarendon Press
Dell	Dell Publishing Co., Inc.	Dodd	Dodd, Mead and Co.
Doubleday	Doubleday and Co., Inc.	Dover	Dover Publications, Inc.
Dutton	E. P. Dutton, Inc.	Funk	Funk and Wagnalls, Inc.
GPO	Government Printing Office	Harcourt	Harcourt Brace Jovanovich, Inc.
Harper	Harper and Row, Publishers, Inc.	Holt	Holt, Rinehart, and Winston, Inc.
Houghton	Houghton Mifflin Co.	Knopf	Alfred A. Knopf, Inc.
Lippincott	J. B. Lippincott Co.	Little	Little, Brown and Co.
McDougal	McDougal Littell Inc.	McGraw	McGraw-Hill, Inc.
Macmillan	Macmillan Publishing Co., Inc.	MLA	The Modern Language Association of America
Norton	W. W. Norton and Co., Inc.	Penguin	Penguin Books, Inc.
Pocket	Pocket Books	Prentice	Prentice-Hall, Inc.
Putnam's	G. P. Putnam's Sons	Rand	Rand McNally and Co.
Random	Random House, Inc.		
Reader's	Reader's Digest Association	St. Martin's	St. Martin's Press, Inc.
Scott	Scott, Foresman and Co.	Simon	Simon and Schuster, Inc.
Twayne	Twayne Publishers	Viking	The Viking Press, Inc.

Sacred Works and Literary Works

For abbreviations of parts of the Bible and other scriptures, consult a dictionary. For standard abbreviations of works by Shakespeare and other classic works of literature, see the *MLA Handbook for Writers of Research Papers.*

Other Abbreviations for Use in Documentation

The following abbreviations, in addition to the ones given on the preceding pages, are commonly used in documentation.

abr.	abridged	ch.	chapter
chs.	chapters	col.	column

cols.	columns	comp.	compiled by, compiler comps. compilers
cond.	conducted by, conductor	dir.	directed by, director
ed.	edited by, editor, edition	eds.	editors, editions
et al.	*et alii, et aliae* ("and others")	fig.	figure
fwd.	foreword, foreword by	illus.	illustrated by, illustrator, illustration
introd.	introduced by, introduction	n.d.	no date
no.	number	n.p.	no place, no publisher
P	Press	p.	page
par.	paragraph	pp.	pages
qtd.	quoted	rev.	revised by, revision
rpt.	reprinted by, reprint	sc.	scene
sec.	section	ser.	series
trans.	translated by, translator, translation	U	University
		UP	University Press
vers.	version	vol.	volume
vols.	volumes	writ.	written by, writer

APPENDIX C

Forms for Working Bibliography and Works Cited Entries

The following are some basic forms for bibliographic entries. Use these forms on the bibliography cards that make up your Working Bibliography and in the list of Works Cited that appears at the end of your paper.

Whole Books

The following models can also be used for reports and pamphlets.

A. **One author**

Ruiz, Ramón Eduardo. <u>Triumphs and Tragedy: A History of the Mexican People</u>. New York: Norton, 1992.

B. **Two authors**

Gilbert, Sandra M., and Susan Gubar. <u>The Madwoman in the Attic: The Woman Writer and the Nineteenth-Century Literary Imagination</u>. New Haven: Yale UP, 1979.

C. **Three authors**

Demko, George J., Jerome Agel, and Eugene Boe. <u>Why in the World: Adventures in Geography</u>. New York: Anchor-Doubleday, 1992.

D. **Four or more authors**

The abbreviation *et al.* means "and others." Use *et al.* instead of listing all the authors.

Gatto, Joseph, et al. <u>Exploring Visual Design</u>. 2nd ed. Worcester: Davis, 1987.

82

E. No author given

Literary Market Place: The Directory of the American
    Book Publishing Industry. 1992 ed. New York:
    Bowker, 1991.

F. An editor, but no single author

Nabokov, Peter, ed. Native American Testimony: A
    Chronicle of Indian-White Relations from Prophecy
    to the Present, 1492-1992. New York: Viking-
    Penguin, 1991.

G. Two or three editors

Pryor, Karen, and Kenneth S. Norris, eds. Dolphin
    Societies: Discoveries and Puzzles. Berkeley: U
    of California P, 1991.

H. Four or more editors

The abbreviation *et al.* means "and others." Use *et al.* instead of listing all the editors.

McFarlan, Donald, et al., eds. The Guinness Book of
    Records 1992. New York: Facts on File, 1991.

I. An author and a translator

Soseki, Natsume. Kokoro: A Novel and Selected Essays.
    Trans. Edwin McClellan and Jay Rubin. New York:
    Madison, 1992.

J. An author, a translator, and an editor

Capellanus, Andreas. The Art of Courtly Love. Abr.
    ed. Trans. John J. Parry. Ed. Frederick W.
    Locke. New York: Ungar, 1976.

K. A particular edition of a book

Janson, H. W., and Anthony F. Janson. History of Art
    for Young People. 4th ed. New York: Abrams,
    1992.

L. A book or monograph that is part of a series

LaRusso, Carol Spenard, comp. <u>The Green Thoreau</u>. The
    Classic Wisdom Ser. San Rafael: New World
    Library, 1992.

M. A multivolume work

If you have used only one volume of a multivolume work, cite only that volume.

Child, Francis James, ed. <u>The English and Scottish</u>
    <u>Popular Ballads</u>. 1883-98. Vol 1. New York:
    Dover, 1965. 2 vols.

If you have used more than one volume of a multivolume work, cite the entire work.

Child, Francis James, ed. <u>The English and Scottish</u>
    <u>Popular Ballads</u>. 1883-98. 2 vols. New York:
    Dover, 1965.

N. A volume with its own title that is part of a multivolume work with a different title

Durant, Will, and Ariel Durant. <u>Rousseau and</u>
    <u>Revolution: A History of Civilization in France,</u>
    <u>England, and Germany from 1756, and in the</u>
    <u>Remainder of Europe from 1715, to 1789</u>. New York:
    Simon, 1967. Vol. 10 of <u>The Story of</u>
    <u>Civilization</u>. 11 vols. 1935-75.

O. A republished book or a literary work available in several editions

Give the date of the original publication after the title. Then give complete publication information, including the date of the edition that you have used.

Steinbeck, John. <u>The Grapes of Wrath</u>. 1939. New
    York: Penguin, 1976.

P. A government publication

Give the name of the government (country or state). Then give the department if applicable, followed by the agency if applicable. Next give the title, followed by the author if known. Then give the publication information. The publisher of U.S. government documents is usually the Government Printing Office, or GPO.

United States. U.S. Dept. of Education. Office of
        Educational Research and Improvement. <u>OERI</u>
        <u>Publications Guide</u>. By Lance Ferderer.
        Washington: GPO, 1990.

---. ---. ---. Educational Resources Information
        Center. <u>Recent Department of Education</u>
        <u>Publications in ERIC</u>. Washington: GPO, 1992.

Parts of Books

A. A poem, short story, essay, or chapter in a collection of works by one author

Cather, Willa. "Joseph and His Brothers." <u>Cather:</u>
        <u>Stories, Poems, and Other Writings</u>. Comp. Sharon
        O'Brien. New York: Viking, 1992. 859-71.

B. A poem, short story, essay, or chapter in a collection of works by several authors

West, Paul. "Pelé." <u>The Norton Book of Sports</u>. Ed.
        George Plimpton. New York: Norton, 1992. 308.

C. A novel or play in a collection under one cover

Simmons, Alexander. <u>Sherlock Holmes and the Hands of</u>
        <u>Othello</u>. <u>Black Thunder: An Anthology of</u>
        <u>Contemporary African American Drama</u>. Ed. William
        B. Branch. New York: Mentor, 1992. 359-415.

D. An introduction, preface, foreword, or afterword written by the author(s) of a work

Pinson, Linda, and Jerry Jinnett. Dedication. <u>The</u>
        <u>Woman Entrepreneur</u>. Ed. Pinson and Jinnett.
        Tustin: Out of Your Mind, 1992. N.p.

E. An introduction, preface, foreword, or afterword written by someone other than the author(s) of a work

```
Coles, Robert.  Foreword.  No Place to Be: Voices of
     Homeless Children.  By Judith Berck.  Boston:
     Houghton, 1992.  1-4.
```

F. Cross-references

If you have used more than one work from a collection, you may give a complete entry for the collection. Then, in the separate entries for the works, you can refer to the entry for the whole collection by using the editor's last name or, if you have listed more than one work by that editor, the editor's last name and a shortened version of the title.

```
French, Warren, ed.  A Companion to The Grapes of
     Wrath.  New York: Viking, 1963.

---.  "What Did John Steinbeck Know About the 'Okies'?"
     French, Companion 51-53.

Steinbeck, John.  Their Blood Is Strong.  San
     Francisco: Lubin, 1938.  Rpt. in French, Companion
     53-92.
```

G. A reprinted article or essay (one previously published elsewhere)

If a work that appears in a collection first appeared in another place, give complete information for the original publication, followed by "Rpt. in" and complete information for the collection.

```
Searle, John.  "What Is a Speech Act?" Philosophy in
     America.  Ed. Max Black.  London: Allen, 1965.
     221-39.  Rpt. in Readings in the Philosophy of
     Language.  Ed. Jay F. Rosenberg and Charles
     Travis.  Englewood Cliffs: Prentice, 1971.  614-
     28.
```

Magazines, Journals, Newspapers, Encyclopedias, and Newsletters

A. An article in a magazine, journal, or newspaper

```
Smith, Shelley. "Baseball's Forgotten Pioneers." Sports
     Illustrated 30 Mar. 1992: 72.

Schwartz, Felice N. "Women as a Business Imperative."
     Harvard Business Review 70.2 (1992): 105-13.

"Kozyrev's Mission to Washington." Editorial. Boston
     Globe 14 June 1992: 78.
```

If no author is given, begin with the article title. If an author is given, begin with the author's name followed by the article title. When an article continues on a different, non-consecutive page, use a plus sign (+) after the number of the page on which it begins.

B. An article in an encyclopedia or other alphabetically organized reference work

Give the title of the article, the name of the reference work, and the year of the edition.

```
"Zuni." Encyclopaedia Britannica: Micropaedia. 1992 ed.
```

C. A review

```
Kellow, Brian. Rev. of Don Pasquale. Metropolitan Opera
     Guild Education Department. Columbia U Kathryn
     Bache Miller Theater, New York. Opera News June
     1992: 52.
```

If the review is unsigned, begin with *Rev. of* and the title.

D. An article in a newsletter

Follow the basic format for a magazine article or a journal article, depending on whether the newsletter has volume numbers. After the title of the newsletter, add the name of the organization that produces it.

```
Veilleux, Peter. "Amazonian Marchers Climb to Capital"
     Oxfam America News. Oxfam America, Summer 1992: 1+
```

Media and Other Sources

A. An interview that you have conducted or letter you have received

```
Jackson, Jesse. Personal interview (or Letter to the
     author). 15 July 1992.
```

B. A film

```
The Grapes of Wrath. Screenplay by Nunnally Johnson.
     Dir. John Ford. Perf. John Carradine, Jane Darwell,
     and Henry Fonda. Twentieth Century-Fox, 1940.
```

C. A work of art

```
Catlin, George. Four Bears, Second Chief, in Full
     Dress. National Museum of American Art,
     Smithsonian Institution, Washington.
```

D. A television program

Give the episode name (if applicable) and the series or program name. Include any information that you have about the program's writer and director. Then give the network, the local station, the city, and the date the program aired.

```
"A Desert Blooming." Writ. Marshall Riggan. Living
     Wild. Dir. Harry L. Gorden. PBS. WTTW, Chicago.
     29 Apr. 1984.
```

E. A musical composition

```
Chopin, Frédéric. Waltz in A-flat major, op. 42.
```

F. A recording (compact disc, LP, or audiocassette)

If the recording is not a compact disc, include *LP* or *Audiocassette* before the manufacturer's name.

```
Guthrie, Woody. "Do-Re-Me." Dust Bowl Ballads. Compact
     disc. Rounder, 1988.
```

G. A lecture, speech, or address

Give the name of the speaker followed by the name of the speech, if available, or the kind of speech *(Lecture, Introduction, Address)*. Then give the event, the place, and the date.

```
Benjamin, John. Address. First Annual Abolitionist
    March and Rally. Boston, 18 July 1992.
```

Electronic Media

Because the number of electronic information sources is great and increasing rapidly, please refer to the most current edition of the MLA Handbook for Writers of Research Papers *if you need more complete information.*

Portable databases (CD-ROMS, videodiscs, diskettes, and videocassettes)

These products contain fixed information (information that cannot be changed unless a new version is produced and released). Citing them in a research paper is similar to citing printed sources. You should include the following:

- Name of the author, if applicable
- Title of the part of the work, if applicable (Underlined or in quotation marks)
- Title of the product or database (underlined)
- Edition, release, or version, if applicable
- Publication medium (CD-ROM, videodisc, diskette, or videocassette)
- City of publication
- Name of the publisher
- Year of publication

If you cannot find some of this information, cite what is available.

```
Boyer, Paul S., et al. "Troubled Agriculture." The
    Enduring Vision: A History of the American People.
    Interactive Edition. Vers.1.1. CD-ROM. Lexington:
    Heath, 1993.

"Steinbeck's Dust Bowl Saga." Our Times Multimedia
    Encyclopedia of the 20th Century. 1996 ed. CD-ROM.
    Redwood City: Vicarious, 1995.

"The Dust Bowl." In Perspective: Literary Themes in the
    Real World. Videodisc. Evanston: McDougal, 1995.

Eyes on the Prize. Prod. Blackside. 6 episodes.
    Videocassettes. PBS Video, 1986.
```

Online Databases

Because online databases may be updated or changed frequently, it is important to include complete information when citing them.

- Name of the author, if applicable
- Title of the material accessed (in quotation marks)
- Date of the material if applicable
- Title of the database (underlined)
- Publication medium *(online)*
- Name of the computer service or computer network (e.g., Prodigy, Internet)
- Date of access (the date you found the information online)

> "Drought." <u>Compton's Living Encyclopedia</u>. Online. America Online. 18 Dec. 1995.

> "Nebraska data." <u>1990 Census Lookup</u>. Online. Internet. 8 Jan. 1996.

> "Great North American Prairie Ecoregion." <u>Sierra Club Foundation</u>. Online. Internet. 19 Dec. 1995.

> Dickens, Charles. <u>A Christmas Carol</u>. London: Chapman and Hall, 1893. Online. Oxford Text Archive. Internet. 19 Dec. 1995.

> Whitman, Walt. <u>Leaves of Grass</u>. Philadelphia: McKay, 1900. Online. Columbia U Academic Information Systems. Internet. 19 Dec. 1995.

Electronic texts of many literary works and historical documents are available online. You should be aware that not all texts are equally reliable. Try to use a text that gives the title, editor, and date of the publication of the work. Include the following in your citation:

- Name of the author, if applicable
- Title of the text (underlined)
- Publication information for the printed source.
- Publication medium *(Online)*
- Name of the repository of the electronic text (e.g., Oxford Text Archive)
- Name of the computer network
- Date of access (the date you found the information online)

Alternative Documentation Styles

The documentation style suggested in this book, which involves parenthetical citations and a list of Works Cited, is recommended by the *MLA Handbook for Writers of Research Papers* and is widely used for work in language, literature, the arts, and the humanities throughout the English-speaking world. However, other approaches to documentation are possible. One common approach is to use endnotes or footnotes in place of parenthetical citations.

Endnote and Footnote Style

Some people prefer endnotes or footnotes because they remove the clutter of citations from the text of the research paper. Instead of a citation, what appears in the text is a number placed after a sentence and above the line, as follows:

```
Colonel Shaw's mother is said to have cried from

happiness on seeing her son at the head of the all-

African-American 54th Massachusetts.[5]
```

The number that is placed above the line is called a **superscript.** Throughout the paper, each instance of material taken from a source is marked with such a superscript. The superscript refers the reader to a note that appears either at the bottom of the page on which the superscript appears or at the end of the paper. If the note appears at the bottom of the page, it is called a **footnote.** If it appears at the end of the paper, it is called an **endnote.** Footnotes have become unpopular in recent years because of their tendency to clutter the pages of a paper. Most writers who use notes instead of parenthetical citations prefer endnotes. The following is a sample endnote or footnote entry:

```
5 Shelby Foote, Fredericksburg to Meridian (New York:
Vintage-Random, 1986) 697, vol. 2 of The Civil War: A
Narrative, 3 vols., 1958-74.
```

An endnote or footnote differs from a Working Bibliography or Works Cited entry in the following ways:

1. The first line of a Working Bibliography or Works Cited entry begins at the left margin. The first line of an endnote or footnote is indented five spaces.

2. Subsequent lines of a Working Bibliography or Works Cited entry are indented five spaces. Subsequent lines of an endnote or footnote begin at the left margin.

3. A Working Bibliography or Works Cited entry does not have a superscript at the beginning. An endnote or footnote does.

4. The name at the beginning of a Working Bibliography or Works Cited entry is reversed for alphabetizing. In an endnote or footnote, the name is given in its normal order.

5. A Working Bibliography or Works Cited entry has three main parts, each of which ends with a period: the name, the title, and the publication information. An endnote or footnote has four main parts, only the last of which ends with a period: the name, the title, the publication information, and the page number(s).

For proper placement of endnotes and footnotes, see the samples on pages 109–111. The chart on the following pages gives sample forms for endnotes and footnotes.

Sample Entries for Endnotes and Footnotes

Whole Books

The following models can also be used for reports and pamphlets.

A. One author

¹ Ramón Eduardo Ruiz, <u>Triumphs and Tragedy: A History of the Mexican People</u> (New York: Norton, 1992) 14.

B. Two authors

² Sandra M. Gilbert and Susan Gubar, <u>The Madwoman in the Attic: The Woman Writer and the Nineteenth-Century Literary Imagination</u> (New Haven: Yale UP, 1979) 65.

C. Three authors

³ George J. Demko, Jerome Agel, and Eugene Boe, <u>Why in the World: Adventures in Geography</u> (New York: Anchor-Doubleday, 1992) 15-16.

D. Four or more authors

The abbreviation *et al.* means "and others." Use *et al.* instead of listing all the authors.

⁴ Joseph Gatto, et al., <u>Exploring Visual Design</u>, 2nd ed. (Worcester: Davis, 1987) 43.

E. No author given

⁵ <u>Literary Market Place: The Directory of the American Book Publishing Industry</u>, 1992 ed. (New York: Bowker, 1991) 1673.

F. An editor, but no single author

⁶ Peter Nabokov, ed., <u>Native American Testimony: A Chronicle of Indian-White Relations from Prophecy to the Present, 1492-1992</u> (New York: Viking-Penguin, 1991) 101.

G. Two or three editors

⁷ Karen Pryor and Kenneth S. Norris, eds., <u>Dolphin</u>

<u>Societies: Discoveries and Puzzles</u> (Berkeley: U of California P, 1991) 36.

H. Four or more editors

The abbreviation *et al.* means "and others." Use *et al.* instead of listing all the editors.

    [8] Donald McFarlan, et al., eds., <u>The Guinness Book of Records 1992</u> (New York: Facts on File, 1991) 99.

I. An author and a translator

    [9] Natsume Soseki, <u>Kokoro: A Novel and Selected Essays</u>, trans. Edwin McClellan and Jay Rubin (New York: Madison, 1992) 115.

J. An author, a translator, and an editor

    [10] Andreas Capellanus, <u>The Art of Courtly Love</u>, abr. ed., trans. John J. Parry, ed. Frederick W. Locke (New York: Ungar, 1976) 42.

K. A particular edition of a book

    [11] H. W. Janson and Anthony F. Janson, <u>History of Art for Young People</u>, 4th ed. (New York: Abrams, 1992) 45.

L. A book or monograph that is part of a series

    [12] Carol Spenard LaRusso, comp., <u>The Green Thoreau</u>, The Classic Wisdom Ser. (San Rafael: New World Library, 1992) 47.

M. A multivolume work

If you are referring to a particular place in one volume, use this form:

    [13] Francis James Child, ed., <u>The English and Scottish Popular Ballads</u>, vol. 1 (1883-98; New York: Dover, 1965) 22.

Endnotes and footnotes that refer to entire works are quite rare. However, if you are referring to an entire multivolume work, use the following form, with no page number.

    [14] Francis James Child, ed., <u>The English and Scottish Popular Ballads</u>, 2 vols. (1883-98; New York: Dover, 1965).

N. A volume with its own title that is part of a multivolume work with a different title

15 Will Durant and Ariel Durant, <u>Rousseau and Revolution: A History of Civilization in France, England, and Germany from 1756, and in the Rest of Europe from 1715, to 1789</u> (New York: Simon, 1967) 18, vol. 10 of <u>The Story of Civilization</u>, 11 vols, 1935-75.

O. A republished book or a literary work available in several editions

Give the date of the orginal publication before the complete publication information. Then, after the place of publication, give the date for the edition that you have used.

16 John Steinbeck, <u>The Grapes of Wrath</u> (1939; New York: Penguin, 1989) 339.

P. A government publication

Give the name of the government (country or state). Then give the department, if applicable, followed by the agency, if applicable. Next give the title, followed by the author, if known. Then give the publication information. The publisher of U.S. government documents is usually the Government Printing Office, or GPO.

17 United States, U.S. Dept. of Education, Office of Educational Research and Improvement, <u>OERI Publications Guide</u>, by Lance Ferderer (Washington: GPO, 1990) 27.

18 ---, ---, ---, Educational Resources Information Center, <u>Recent Department of Education Publications in ERIC</u> (Washington: GPO, 1992) 162.

Parts of Books

A. A poem, short story, essay, or chapter in a collection of works by one author

19 Willa Cather, "Joseph and His Brothers," <u>Cather: Stories, Poems, and Other Writings</u>, comp. Sharon O'Brien (New York: Viking, 1992) 860.

B. A poem, short story, essay, or chapter in a collection of works by several authors

20 Paul West, "Pelé," <u>The Norton Book of Sports</u>, ed. George Plimpton (New York: Norton, 1992) 308.

C. A novel or play in a collection under one cover

21 Alexander Simmons, <u>Sherlock Holmes and the Hands of Othello</u>, <u>Black Thunder: An Anthology of Contemporary African American Drama</u>, ed. William B. Branch (New York: Mentor, 1992) 411.

D. An introduction, preface, foreword, or afterword written by the author(s) of a work

22 Linda Pinson and Jerry Jinnett, dedication, <u>The Woman Entrepreneur</u>, ed. Pinson and Jinnett (Tustin: Out of Your Mind, 1992) n.p.

E. An introduction, preface, foreword, or afterword written by someone other than the author(s) of a work

23 Robert Coles, foreword, <u>No Place to Be: Voices of Homeless Children</u>, by Judith Berck (Boston: Houghton, 1992) 2.

F. A reprinted article or essay (one previously published elsewhere)

If a work that appears in a collection first appeared in another place, give complete information for the original publication, followed by "rpt. in" and complete information for the collection.

24 John Searle, "What Is a Speech Act?" <u>Philosophy in America</u>, ed. Max Black (London: Allen, 1965) 221–39, rpt. in <u>Readings in the Philosophy of Language</u>, ed. Jay F. Rosenberg and Charles Travis (Englewood Cliffs: Prentice, 1971) 615.

Magazines, Journals, Newspapers, Encyclopedias, and Newsletters

A. An article in a magazine, journal, or newspaper

25 Shelley Smith, "Baseball's Forgotten Pioneers,"

<u>Sports Illustrated</u> 30 Mar. 1992: 72.

    26 Felice N. Schwartz, "Women as a Business
Imperative," <u>Harvard Business Review</u> 70.2 (1992): 105-13.

    27 "Kozyrev's Mission to Washington," editorial, <u>Boston
Globe</u> 14 June 1992: 78.

If no author is given, begin with the article title. If an author is given, begin with the author's name followed by the article title. When an article continues on a different, non-consecutive page, use a plus sign (+) after the number of the page on which it begins.

B. An article in an encyclopedia or other alphabetically organized reference work

Give the title of the article, the name of the reference work, and the year of the edition.

    28 "Zuni," <u>Encyclopaedia Britannica: Micropaedia</u>, 1992
ed.

C. A review

    29 Brian Kellow, rev. of <u>Don Pasquale</u>, Metropolitan
Opera Guild Education Department, Columbia U Kathryn Bache
Miller Theater, New York, <u>Opera News</u> June 1992: 52.

If the review is unsigned, begin with *Rev. of* and the title.

D. An article in a newsletter

Follow the basic format for a magazine article or a journal article, depending on whether the newsletter has volume numbers. After the title of the newsletter, add the name of the organization that produces it.

    30 Veilleux, Peter, "Amazonian Marchers Climb to
Capital," <u>Oxfam America News</u>, Oxfam America, Summer 1992: 1+

Media and Other Sources

A. An interview that you have conducted or letter you have received

    31 Jesse Jackson, personal interview (*or* letter to the
author), 15 July 1992.

B. A film

 [32] <u>The Grapes of Wrath</u>, screenplay by Nunnally Johnson, perf. John Carradine, Jane Darwell, and Henry Fonda, Twentieth Century-Fox, 1940.

C. A work of art

 [33] George Catlin, <u>Four Bears, Second Chief, in Full Dress</u>. National Museum of American Art, Smithsonian Institution, Washington.

D. A television program

Give the episode name (if applicable) and the series or program name. Include any information that you have about the program's writer and director. Then give the network, the local station, the city, and the date the program aired.

 [34] "A Desert Blooming," writ. Marshall Riggan, <u>Living Wild</u>, dir. Harry L. Gorden, PBS, WTTW, Chicago, 29 Apr. 1984.

E. A musical composition

 [35] Frédéric Chopin, Waltz in A-flat major, op. 42.

F. A recording (compact disc, LP, or audiocassette)

If the recording is not a compact disc, include *LP* or *Audiocassette* before the manufacturer's name.

 [36] Woody Guthrie, "Do-Re-Me," <u>Dust Bowl Ballads</u>, compact disc, Rounder, 1988.

G. A lecture, speech or address

Give the name of the speaker followed by the name of the speech, if available, or the kind of speech *(Lecture, Introduction, Address)*. Then give the event, the place, and the date.

 [37] John Benjamin, address, First Annual Abolitionist March and Rally, Boston, 18 July 1992.

Electronic Media

Because the number of electronic information sources is great and increasing rapidly,

98

please refer to the most current edition of the MLA Handbook for Writers of Research Papers *if you need more complete information.*

Portable databases (CD-ROMS, videodiscs, diskettes, and videocassettes)

These products contain fixed information (information that cannot be changed unless a new version is produced and released). Citing them in a research paper is similar to citing printed sources. You should include the following:

- Name of the author, if applicable
- Title of the part of the work, if applicable (underlined or in quotation marks)
- Title of the product or database (underlined)
- Edition, release, or version, if applicable
- Publication medium (CD-ROM, videodisc, diskette, or videocassette)
- City of publication
- Name of the publisher
- Year of publication

If you cannot find some of this information, cite what is available.

[38] Paul S. Boyer, et al, "Troubled Agriculture," The Enduring Vision: A History of the American People, Interactive Edition, Vers.1.1, CD-ROM (Lexington: Heath, 1993).

[39] "Steinbeck's Dust Bowl Saga," Our Times Multimedia Encyclopedia of the 20th Century, 1996 ed., CD-ROM (Redwood City: Vicarious, 1995).

[40] "The Dust Bowl." In Perspective: Literary Themes in the Real World, videodisc (Evanston: McDougal, 1995).

[41] Eyes on the Prize, prod. Blackside, 6 episodes, videocassettes. PBS Video, 1986.

Online Databases

Because online databases may be updated or changed frequently, it is important to include complete information when citing them. You cannot know that the information you find will be the same when someone else looks for it. You should include the following:

- Name of the author, if applicable

- Title of the material accessed (in quotation marks)
- Date of the material if applicable
- Title of the database (underlined)
- Publication medium *(online)*
- Name of the computer service or computer network (e.g., CompuServe, America Online, Prodigy, Internet)
- Date of access (the date you found the information online)

42 "Drought," <u>Compton's Living Encyclopedia</u>, online, America Online, 18 Dec. 1995.

43 "Nebraska data," <u>1990 Census Lookup</u>, online, Internet, 8 Jan. 1996.

44 "Great North American Prairie Ecoregion," <u>Sierra Club Foundation</u>, online, Internet, 19 Dec. 1995.

Electronic texts of many literary works and historical documents are available online (often through universities and government agencies). You should be aware that not all texts are equally reliable. Try to use a text that gives the title, editor, and date of the publication of the work. Check with a librarian or your teacher if you have questions about the reliability of online sources. You should include the following.

- Name of the author, if applicable
- Title of the text (underlined)
- Publication information for the printed source.
- Publication medium *(online)*
- Name of the repository of the electronic text (e.g., Oxford Text Archive)
- Name of the computer network
- Date of access (the date you found the information online)

45 Charles Dickens, <u>A Christmas Carol</u>. (London: Chapman and Hall, 1893), online, Oxford Text Archive, Internet, 19 Dec. 1995.

46 Walt Whitman, <u>Leaves of Grass</u>. (Philadelphia, McKay, 1900), online, Columbia U Academic Information Systems, Internet, 19 Dec. 1995.

Subsequent References

The first time that you write an endnote or footnote for a work, give a full entry. Thereafter, you can give the author's or editor's name by itself.

⁵¹ Warren French, "What Did John Steinbeck Know About the 'Okies'?" <u>A Companion to</u> The Grapes of Wrath, ed. French (New York: Viking, 1963) 52.

⁵² French 53.

If you have cited more than one work by the author or editor, then include shortened forms of the titles in subsequent endnotes or footnotes:

⁵³ French, "What Did" 53.

Other Types of Documentation

Two other documentation styles are in widespread use today. The **author-date** system is used widely in the sciences. This system is like the standard parenthetical citation system but includes, after the author's or editor's last name, the date of publication, a comma, and the page number.

> Colonel Shaw's mother is said to have cried from
>
> happiness on seeing her son at the head of the all-
>
> African-American 54th Massachusetts (Foote 1986,
>
> 697).

In the author-date system, the form of Works Cited entries is the same as in the standard parenthetical citation system, with the exception that the date of publication is given immediately after the author's or editor's name.

Foote, Shelby. 1986. <u>Fredericksburg to Meridian</u>. New

York: Vintage-Random. Vol. 2 of <u>The Civil War: A</u>

<u>Narrative</u>. 3 vols. 1958-74.

If the Works Cited list contains more than one work published by the same author or editor in the same year, then lowercase letters (a, b, c, and so on) are used to distinguish the works:

```
Colonel Shaw's mother is said to have cried from

happiness on seeing her son at the head of the all-

African-American 54th Massachusetts (Foote 1986a,

697).
```

Foote, Shelby. 1986a. Fredericksburg to Meridian. New

    York: Vintage-Random. Vol. 2 of The Civil War: A

    Narrative. 3 vols. 1958-74.

In the **number system** of documentation, each entry in the list of Works Cited is numbered with an Arabic numeral (1, 2, 3, and so on). The entries in the list of Works Cited can be arranged in any order that is useful, such as chronological order or the order in which the works are cited in the research paper.

1. Foote, Shelby. Fredericksburg to Meridian. New York:

    Vintage-Random, 1986. Vol. 2 of The Civil War: A

    Narrative. 3 vols. 1958-74.

2. Benjamin, John. Address. First Annual Abolitionist

    March and Rally. Boston, 18 July 1992.

A parenthetical citation in the text of the research paper consists of the number of the Works Cited entry, underlined; a comma; and the page number.

```
Colonel Shaw's mother is said to have cried from hap-
```

```
piness on seeing her son at the head of the all-

African-American 54th Massachusetts (1, 697).
```

Other Style Manuals

The documentation style used in this book is that of the *MLA Handbook for Writers of Research Papers*. Other styles are often followed in the sciences. Here is a list of style manuals commonly used by people doing scientific and mathematical research in the United States:

CBE Style Manual: A Guide for Authors, Editors, and Publishers in the Biological Sciences

Handbook for Authors of Papers in American Chemical Society Publications

A Manual for Authors of Mathematical Papers

Publication Manual of the American Psychological Association

Suggestions to Authors of the Reports of the United States Geological Survey

Another style manual that is widely used in a variety of fields, especially in the humanities, is *The Chicago Manual of Style*.

This is a sample paper done in endnote style. For a sample done in footnote style, see page 111.

Marcus Washington

Mr. Zacharis

American History

3 May 1993

The "Victory" of the Massachusetts 54th

at Fort Wagner

On Boston Common, near the Massachusetts State House, stands an impressive monument--a sculpture depicting a group of African-American soldiers marching in the uniforms of the Union Army.[1] This monument commemorates the brave men of the Massachusetts 54th Infantry Regiment, who on July 18, 1863, at the height of the Civil War, stormed a South Carolina earthwork known as Fort Wagner or Battery Wagner. When the fighting was done, nearly half of those men lay dead in what was by all accounts a massacre, an overwhelming victory for the Confederacy.[2] However, the events at Fort Wagner were strangely contradictory. Although many Yankee soldiers lost their lives in the charge, and although the Confederates technically won the battle, one can rightly claim that the battle was a great victory for the Union Army and for all people of color.

The first calls for recruitment of African-American soldiers into the Union Army came from abolitionist leaders. Frederick Douglass, the charismatic African-American orator, newspaper editor, and abolitionist, had proclaimed, "The arm of the slaves [is] the best defense against the arm of the slaveholder. . . . Who would be free themselves must strike the blow."[3] Wendell Phillips, a leader of the Boston abolitionists, had declared, "We have given the sword to the white man; the time has come to give it to the black!"[4] According to historian Barbara Fields, a convention of free African Americans meeting in 1863 resolved: "It is time now

Note that endnote numbers appear **superscripted**, or slightly raised above the line.

The brackets enclose a slight modification made to the source in order to fit it grammatically into the paper.

for more effective remedies to be thoroughly tried in the
shape of warm lead and cold steel duly administered by 100,000
black doctors."[5] By that time, Congress had authorized the
enlistment of African-American troops, a move that met with
the full support of Ulysses S. Grant:

> I have given the subject of arming the Negro my
> hearty support. This, with the emancipation of the
> Negro, is the heaviest blow yet given the
> Confederacy. . . . [W]e have added a powerful ally.
> They will make good soldiers and taking them from
> the enemy weakens him in the same proportion they
> strengthen us.[6]

The African-American 54th Massachusetts Infantry Regiment
was the brainchild of Governor John A. Andrew, who on January
26, 1863, had responded to Lincoln's Emancipation Proclamation
by writing to Edwin Stanton, Lincoln's secretary of war,
requesting permission to raise a regiment of troops of
African-American descent.[7] To lead the regiment, Andrew chose
a young soldier named Robert Gould Shaw, from a staunchly
antislavery family in Boston.[8] By May 14, one thousand men
had volunteered to serve in the 54th.[9] For some time,
however, the Union commanders were reluctant to put their
African-American troops into combat.[10] On July 6, Colonel
Shaw wrote to Brigadier General George C. Strong, complaining
that his men were not being put to use.[11] On July 18, Shaw
and his regiment got their chance to see action.

Fort Wagner, "perhaps the strongest [earthwork] ever
built," sat on the Atlantic coast at the mouth of Charleston
Harbor. Taking Fort Wagner was part of the Union Army's
overall plan to take the city of Charleston.[12] Unfortunately
for the Union troops, the only approach to the fort was a
narrow area less than two hundred yards wide.[13] Any troops

Note that an endnote
number is placed
outside a final
quotation mark.

A long quotation is set
off from the text and
indented ten spaces.
The endnote number
follows the end of the
quotation.

crossing that area would be in grave danger from the Confederate troops stationed inside the fort. Colonel Shaw enthusiastically agreed to lead the attack on Fort Wagner.[14] The attack began at 7:30 at night:

> The 1000-man rebel garrison came out of the bombproof to which it had retired at the height of the cannonade and met the attackers. . . . When flesh and blood could stand no more, the survivors fell back from the ditch and parapet, black and white alike, and returned to the trenches they had left an hour ago. Casualties had been heavy; 1515 of the attackers had fallen, as compared to 174 of the defenders. . . . [N]ext morning . . . a brief truce sufficed for removal of the wounded and disposal of the slain, including the twenty-six-year-old Shaw.[15]

It was a terrible defeat, and yet there are two reasons for considering it a victory as well. The first reason is that the charge gave the men of the 54th helped to create an attitude both within them and within many whites that would make it difficult for any Americans of African descent to be made slaves again. The second reason is that the charge proved the value of African-American soldiers and led to their further participation in the war.

The bravery of the 54th Massachusetts proved that African Americans could be good soldiers. After the charge on Fort Wagner, the numbers of African-American enlisted men grew. A total of 180,000 African-American soldiers served with the Union Army during the last years of the war--a force equal to an astonishing 85 percent of the eligible male African-American population.[16]

The charge on Fort Wagner was also a powerful blow against slavery. The institution of slavery depended on the ability of people to believe that some human beings were inherently less capable or less worthy than others. As Confederate general Howell Cobb had put it, "If slaves seem good soldiers, then our whole theory of slavery is wrong."[17] The men of the 54th were determined to prove that the theory was wrong. As one member of the 54th is reported to have said, "We want 'em to know that we went down standing up."[18] By not flinching from their duty, by charging onward against overwhelming odds, the men of the 54th demonstrated their courage and the falsehood of the racist assumption of lesser worth underlying slavery. General William Tecumseh Sherman of the Union forces pointed out, after African-American soldiers took up arms, "They [the South] can't get back their slaves. It is dead."[19] It was the fulfillment of a prophecy that Frederick Douglass had made:

> Once let a black man get upon his person the brass letters, "U.S." . . . [l]et him get an eagle on his buttons and a musket on his shoulder and bullets in his pocket, and there is no power on earth which can deny that he has earned the right to citizenship in the United States.[20]

The charge of the 54th is considered by many African Americans today a critical point in history, a point when their ancestors established their right to citizenship. Monica Fairbanks, director of the Afro-American History Museum in Boston, quotes with approval William Carney, a member of the Massachusetts 54th who was awarded the Congressional Medal of Honor: "We . . . take up arms in defense of a nation to which we belong."[21] State Senator Bill Orin of Massachusetts considers celebration of the memory of the Massachusetts 54th to be equivalent to "celebrating the diversity of the United States of America."[22] John Benjamin of the National Park Service speaks of the importance of having the world recognize "the contribution of the 54th to the freedom of our people."[23] Gloria Fox, a Massachusetts state representative, says, "The struggle continues—-that's what [remembering] the 54th means."[24] Each of these leaders recognizes the charge of the 54th not as a defeat but as a great moral victory--a victory pulled, as the proverb has it, "from the jaws of defeat." That the charge of the Massachusetts 54th is today remembered in this way is a fulfillment of a prediction made by Abraham Lincoln:

> When victory is won, there will be some black men who can remember that, with silent tongue and clenched teeth and steady eye and well-poised bayonet, they have helped mankind on to a great consummation.[25]

Ending with a quotation is one innovative way to conclude a research paper or report.

108

Notes

[1] Augustus Saint-Gaudens, <u>Monument to Robert Gould Shaw and His Regiment</u>, Boston Common, Boston.

[2] Geoffrey Ward, <u>The Civil War: An Illustrated History</u> (New York: Knopf, 1990) 248.

[3] "The Universe of Battle," episode 5 of <u>The Civil War</u>, dir. Ken Burns, writ. Geoffrey C. Ward and Rick Burns with Ken Burns, Florentine Films, 1989.

[4] Peter Burchard, <u>One Gallant Rush: Robert Gould Shaw and His Brave Black Regiment</u> (New York: St. Martin's, 1965) 43.

[5] Ward 246-47.

[6] Ward 247.

[7] Burchard 2.

[8] Burchard 71.

[9] Burchard 90.

[10] Ward 247.

[11] Burchard 117-18.

[12] Burchard 120-21.

[13] Shelby Foote, <u>Fredericksburg to Meridian</u> (New York: Vintage-Random, 1986) 697, vol. 2 of <u>The Civil War: A Narrative</u>, 3 vols., 1954-78.

[14] Burchard 133.

[15] Foote 697.

[16] "Universe."

[17] Qtd. in Ward 253.

[18] <u>Glory</u>, dir. Edward Zwick, prod. Freddie Fields, with Matthew Broderick and Denzel Washington, Tri-Star, 1989.

[19] Qtd. in "Universe."

[20] Qtd. in Ward 246.

[21] Monica Fairbanks, personal interview, 18 July 1992.

[22] Bill Orin, address, First Annual Abolitionist March and Rally, Boston, 18 July 1992.

[23] John Benjamin, address, First Annual Abolitionist March and Rally, Boston, 18 July 1992.

[24] Gloria Fox, greetings, Abolitionist Rally at the African Meeting House, 18 July 1992.

[25] Qtd. in "Universe."

Marcus Washington

Mr. Zacharis

American History

3 May 1993

The Victory of the Massachusetts 54th

at Fort Wagner

On Boston Common, near the Massachusetts State House, stands an impressive monument--a sculpture depicting a group of African-American soldiers marching in the uniforms of the Union Army.[1] This monument commemorates the brave men of the Massachusetts 54th Infantry Regiment, who on July 18, 1863, at the height of the Civil War, stormed a South Carolina earthwork known as Fort Wagner or Battery Wagner. When the fighting was done, nearly half of those men lay dead in what was by all accounts a massacre, an overwhelming victory for the Confederacy.[2] However, the events at Fort Wagner were strangely contradictory. Although many Yankee soldiers lost their lives in the charge, and although the Confederates technically won the battle, one can rightly claim that the battle was a great victory for the Union Army and for all people of color.

The first calls for recruitment of African-American soldiers into the Union Army came from abolitionist leaders. Frederick Douglass, the charismatic African-American orator, newspaper editor, and abolitionist, had proclaimed, "The arm

---

1 Augustus Saint-Gaudens, <u>Monument to Robert Gould Shaw and His Regiment</u>, Boston Common, Boston.

2 Geoffrey Ward, <u>The Civil War: An Illustrated History</u> (New York: Knopf, 1990) 248.

111

Index